Whistle-Stop Puppet Plays

WHISTLE-STOP PUPPET PLAYS

by
Taffy Jones

McFarland & Company, Inc., Publishers
Jefferson & London

Front cover photo of Kiel and Kehr Davis and all interior photos by Taffy Jones.

Back cover photo of Taffy Jones by Shirley Tuck.

Library of Congress Cataloguing-in-Publication Data

Jones, Taffy.
  Whistle-stop puppet plays.

  1. Puppets and puppet-plays. I. Title.
PN1980.J58 1983   791.5′3   82-23931

ISBN 0-89950-075-7 (sewn softcover;
  55# acid-free natural paper) ∞

© 1983 Taffy Jones. All rights reserved.

Manufactured in the United States of America

McFarland & Company, Inc., Publishers
  Box 611, Jefferson, North Carolina 28640

To my three grandsons,
Scott, Brian and Trent

Special Thanks to

Victoria S. Johnson, known as the Book Witch, who introduced me to puppetry and made the papier mâché puppets used in the plays, and who made the hand puppets for "Mall E. Mouse" which appear on the front cover.

Carol Reed, for the cloth puppets used in the play "Dusty's Flea Market."

Eunice Pomaville, D.S. Jones, Nancy Leinbach, and Sally Wiedemann for their helpfulness.

Robert Dempster, for the title-page drawing, and Ron Portz, for his how-to drawings.

Art Johnson, for the Cat-Mouse video game prop.

Nancy Henk, Arts, Crafts and Puppetry specialist for the Detroit Recreation Department, for the theatre designs.

Betty Wilkens, librarian of the Martin County Public Library, and the Marco Puppeteers of Stuart, Florida.

"Booker's Bad Dream" was written especially for Bloomfield Township Library, Bloomfield Hills, Mich. (Barbara Klein and Carolyn Nagengast, librarians).

"Booker Is Back" was written for classes in puppetry at Conant Elementary School, Bloomfield Hills, Mich. (Carol Johnson, principal).

"Ghosts in the Pumpkin Patch" was written especially for Farmington Community Center, Farmington Hills, Mich. (Betty Paine, director).

"Papa, Say No!" was especially written for Eriksson Elementary School, Canton, Mich. (Jean Lawrence, librarian and Bill Lutz, principal).

"The Pillhilly Pig" was especially written for Hickory Grove Elementary School, Bloomfield Hills, Mich. (Flo Schermerhorn, teacher).

"Dusty's Flea Market" and "Mall E. Mouse" were written especially for the ABC Day Care Center, Bainbridge, Ohio (Brenda Perry, director, and Kerry King, teacher).

"Booker's Library Party" was written especially for Bryant Branch Public Library, Dearborn, Mich. (Linda McCarty, librarian).

"Old MacDonald Has a Barn" was written especially for Kirk-in-the-Hills Presbyterian Church, Bloomfield Hills, Mich. (Dr. James F. Anderson, pastor).

The children presented all the plays except those at Bloomfield Township Public Library and those presented by the Marco Puppeteers.

Contents

Special Thanks	vi
Introduction	ix
Booker's Bad Dream	1
Booker Puppet	10
Booker Is Back	14
Old MacDonald Has a Barn	22
Country Cousin Puppet	34
Papa, Say No!	38
Alligator Puppet	52
The Pillhilly Pig	56
Hatfields and McCoys Puppets	68
Dusty's Flea Market	70
Flea Puppet	82
Mall E. Mouse	87
Cat-Mouse Video Game	97
Mouse Stick Puppet	98
Ghosts in the Pumpkin Patch	101
Indian Ghost Puppet	113
Booker's Library Party	116
Things to Remember	125
Simple Puppet Stages	127

Introduction

Whistle-Stop Puppet Plays is a book of nine original puppet plays that have been presented in schools, libraries, churches, synagogues, community centers, garages, barns and on television.

The book was written especially for teachers and librarians so they could present the ever-popular puppet play with very little effort and expense in their busy schedules. There are how-to's throughout the book to help guide them, and the plays are flexible enough so they can be added to or subtracted from by the director.

Whistle-Stop Puppet Plays are up-to-date and easy enough for the children to perform. They can be read as a story by adding the "who-said" to the lines. The children can relate to the characters and the situations. They are fun puppet plays to produce and to see: *Whistle-Stop Puppet Plays* is a handy book to have on the library shelf.

Booker's Bad Dream

WHERE: A library shelf. WHEN: Anytime. PUPPETEERS: TWO. TIME: 9 minutes.

CHARACTERS

BOOKER............	A handsome book full of facts and fiction
BOOKWORM........	A library bookworm
RACKET	A noisy parrot
STICKY ICKY	A messy pig
MARKER...........	A marking mouse
CRUSHER..........	An alligator who bites

Note: Any puppet characters can be used instead of the above. BOOKER can be made like a book from a covered cereal box, adding hands and a head. The word BOOKER can be written on the front of the box, and BOOKER again on the back binding. Complete instructions are given. Music can be used before and after the play.

At Rise: Booker is standing on a book shelf in the library. Rows of colorful material, with titles on the bindings, are glued or sewed to the back curtain. A sign which is glued or sewed to the back curtain says, "QUIET PLEASE."

BOOKER: *(Is eating a peanut butter and jelly sandwich.)* Hello my little bookworm friend. Been eating any paste off the library books lately?

BOOKWORM: Now, Booker, you know I don't eat paste off library books. I don't eat the bindings off books, either.

BOOKER: I was only kidding. Hum! This peanut butter and jelly sandwich of mine tastes good.

BOOKWORM: I like peanut butter and jelly sandwiches so much. How many have you eaten, Booker?

BOOKER: Six.

BOOKWORM: Six? Gosh, Booker, don't you know eating too many peanut butter and jelly sandwiches can give you a stomach ache?

BOOKER: No, they won't.

BOOKWORM: Didn't you know eating too many peanut butter and jelly sandwiches can make you have bad dreams?

BOOKER: Stop the fooling, Bookworm.

BOOKWORM: I'm not fooling. They will. Yes, they will.

BOOKER: How do you know?

BOOKWORM: I read it somewhere.

BOOKER: You are always reading something, somewhere.

BOOKWORM: That's why I'm called Bookworm.

BOOKER: You are a bookworm full of knowledge.

BOOKWORM: I try to be.

BOOKER: You know, Bookworm, I am glad the librarian chose me to live in this library. *(The name of your library can be used here.)*

BOOKWORM: Me, too. You are my best friend. You are a special book, full of facts and fiction, mysteries and histories and beeeea-u-tiful pictures.

BOOKER: Thanks, Bookworm. You are special, too, and you are my best friend.

BOOKWORM: I'm so hungry, Booker. *(Looks closely at* BOOKER'S *sandwich.)*

BOOKER: I know you have had your eye on my sandwich. Here, you can have it. *(Puts the sandwich into* BOOKWORM'S *mouth.)* I'm full.

BOOKWORM: Thanks, Booker. *(Mumbles and exits with sandwich in her mouth.)*

BOOKER: Eating all those peanut butter and jelly sandwiches makes me sleepy. *(Stretches his hands.)* I'll take a short nap before the boys and girls come to the library. *(Lies on stage.)* I'm so sleepy. *(Snores.)*

RACKET: *(Enters.)* Wake up, you sleepy head. Gawk! Gawk! *(Loudly.)*

BOOKER: Sh! I'm trying to sleep. Besides, you are supposed to talk soft in the library.

RACKET: I am talking soft.

BOOKER: Well, it's too loud for the library.

RACKET: *(Shouts.)* Oh, crackers!

BOOKER: *(Gets up and points to sign.)* See that sign?

RACKET: What about it?

BOOKER: The sign says, "QUIET PLEASE!"

RACKET: So what does a pretty bird like me care about a silly sign?

BOOKER: *(Whispers.)* You are supposed to whisper in the library.

RACKET: Not me. My voice is too beautiful to hide in a whisper. Squawk! Squawk! *(Very loud.)*

BOOKER: What's your name?

RACKET: My name's Racket. Squawk! Squawk!

BOOKER: *(Covers head with hands.)* You hurt my ears, Racket.

RACKET: *(Struts around making loud noises; keeps on squawking.)* Squawk! Squawk! Squawk! Squawk! Squawk! Squawk!

Booker and Bookworm: two easy-to-make puppets (see instructions for Booker on pages 10–13; for Bookworm, see pages 34–37: Country Worm Cousin and Bookworm are interchangeable).

STICKY ICKY: *(Enters, carrying a big lollipop.)* What is all the terrible racket?

BOOKER: It's Racket.

STICKY ICKY: I know it's a racket. Who's making it?

BOOKER: Racket.

STICKY ICKY: I can't stand the noise. So, out you go, you noisy bird. *(Pushes RACKET off the shelf.)*

BOOKER: I am glad Racket has gone. What's your name?

STICKY ICKY: Sticky Icky is my name. Say, isn't your name Booker?

BOOKER: It is.

STICKY ICKY: I've been wanting to get my hands on you. *(Grabs at BOOKER.)*

BOOKER: *(Backs away.)* You look awfully sticky. You are sticky. You are sticky all over.

STICKY ICKY: It's only marshmallows, mustard, catsup and bubble gum.

BOOKER: Get away from me, Sticky Icky. You will stick my pages together.

STICKY ICKY: My, aren't we fussy? *(Goes to BOOKER.)*

BOOKER: You should wash your hands. You are a dirty pig.

STICKY ICKY: Why bother? They just get dirty again. Oink! Oink! *(Holds BOOKER.)*

BOOKER: Let go of me. Help! Help! You are sticking my pages together.

MARKER: *(Enters carrying a big yellow marker.)* Someone in distress. Need help my good man?

BOOKER: Sticky Icky is sticking my pages together.

MARKER: How ghastly. I will chase that messy pig away. *(Chases STICKY ICKY off the shelf.)* There. Your sticky friend has gone.

BOOKER: Sticky Icky is no friend of mine.

MARKER: I would like to introduce myself. My name is Percival Marker, the Third. Everyone calls me Marker.

BOOKER: My name is Booker T. Learn, but everyone calls me Booker.

MARKER: By jove, you do look interesting. Let's take a peek at you. *(Looks closely at BOOKER.)* Do you mind?

BOOKER: Of course not.

(MARKER marks BOOKER with his marker.)

BOOKER: Hey! What are you doing?

MARKER: *(Keeps marking.)* I'm marking you.

BOOKER: Cut that out. If you keep marking me like that, no one can read me.

MARKER: Picky! Picky! *(Keeps marking.)*

BOOKER: *(Backs away.)* Stop marking me, Marker. You mark out all my words.

MARKER: What a fuss budget. I will mark you all I like.

BOOKER: No, you won't.

MARKER: Yes, I will. *(Chases BOOKER.)*

BOOKER: Go away, Marker. Go away!

MARKER: Nobody escapes the marker. *(Chase continues.)*

CRUSHER: *(Enters.)* What's all the chase?

BOOKER: Marker is marking me so nobody can read me.

CRUSHER: O.K., Marker, leave the guy alone. Quit the marking.

MARKER: Get lost, my good man.

CRUSHER: I am not your good man. *(Opens his mouth wide and shows his sharp teeth.)*

MARKER: Y-Y-You have sharp teeth. Y-Y-You could crush me with one bite.

CRUSHER: Cut the chatter and get lost. *(Moves to MARKER, opening and closing his big mouth.)* Now!

MARKER: I'm going. *(Jumps off the library shelf.)* I'm gone!

BOOKER: Thanks for getting rid of Marker.

CRUSHER: No big deal. Hey, aren't you the Booker everyone's been talking about? Aren't you on the most wanted book list?

BOOKER: The children do like me.

CRUSHER: Yep, you are the Booker I've been wanting to get my jaws on. (*Bites* BOOKER.)

BOOKER: Ouch! You hurt!

CRUSHER: (*Bites again.*) Tough!

BOOKER: Are you going to eat me?

CRUSHER: Naw. I'm just looking you over. (*Pounds on* BOOKER.)

BOOKER: Oh! Oh! You are breaking my back.

CRUSHER: No, I'm not!

BOOKER: Yes, you are, and you are turning down my corners.

CRUSHER: (*Beats on* BOOKER.) What a cry baby!

BOOKER: You are turning my pages so fast you make me dizzy.

CRUSHER: Tough!

BOOKER: You are mean!

CRUSHER: All crushers are mean.

BOOKER: Help! Help! Somebody save me from the crusher.

CRUSHER: Nobody's going to save you.

BOOKER: What will I do?

CRUSHER: You'll have to fight me.

BOOKER: But, I don't believe in fighting.

CRUSHER: Then you'll be torn to shreds.

BOOKER: I don't want to be torn to shreds. (*Faces* CRUSHER *ready to fight.*) So, I'll fight you. I'm not really afraid of you.

CRUSHER: Put up or shut up.

BOOKER: You are a mean looking creature, and you talk mean.

CRUSHER: I like my looks. (*Opens his mouth*). Enough of your talk. I'm going to give you the thrashing of your life.

BOOKER: Oh, no you're not.

CRUSHER: I'm going to rip you apart.

BOOKER: Oh, no you're not.

CRUSHER: I'm going to crush you with my teeth. *(Opens his mouth very wide and rushes at BOOKER.)*

BOOKER: No, you're not! *(Steps aside as CRUSHER rushes at him.)*

(CRUSHER goes off the library shelf.)

BOOKER: I'm glad Crusher has gone.

BOOKWORM: *(Enters.)* Who are you talking to, Booker?

BOOKER: I was talking to mean old Crusher.

BOOKWORM: Crusher?

BOOKER: You should have seen him. He was going to crush me with his sharp teeth.

BOOKWORM: Booker, you've been dreaming.

BOOKER: I guess I have. And, what a bad dream I had. I'm glad I am awake. Gosh, I'm hungry. I'm going to get something to eat. Want to come with me?

BOOKWORM: What are you going to eat, Booker?

BOOKER: Peanut butter and jelly sandwiches, what else? *(They exit.)*

Booker's Bad Dream is a teaching tool for children, and it teaches good library habits. It is a good play for Library Week.

Props: Peanut butter and jelly sandwiches; large lollipop; yellow marker (can be attached to MARKER's hand).

Production Notes: The children can make BOOKER puppets from cereal boxes. The boxes can be covered with bright material. Two holes for hands can be cut out of the box where the children put their thumb and third finger. A styrofoam ball can be used as a head. Felt, or plastic eyes, nose and mouth can be added, or plastic eyes can be pushed into the ball. Yarn hair can be glued to the ball, and BOOKER can wear a tam.

BOOKER's name should be put on the front of the box and also on the back side of the box. The other side of the box can be white felt or cardboard with lines to represent the pages of a closed book.

See instructions for making Booker puppet on pages 10–13.

A Booker

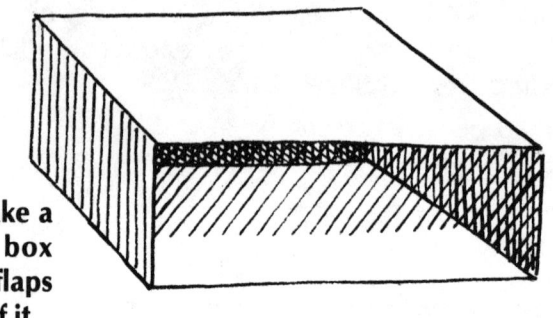

1. To begin, take a small cereal box and cut the flaps from one end of it.

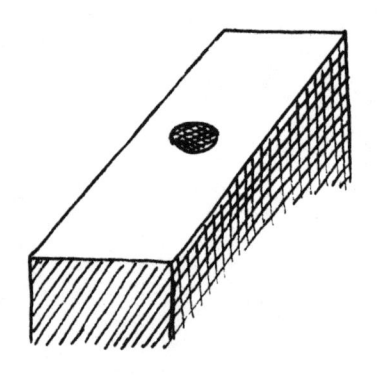

2. Cut a hole the size of a quarter in the top of the box.

3. Make a neck for your puppet by wrapping an index card around your forefinger and taping it.

Booker's Bad Dream 11

4. Then, take a styrofoam ball and make a hole in it with a closed ballpoint pen.

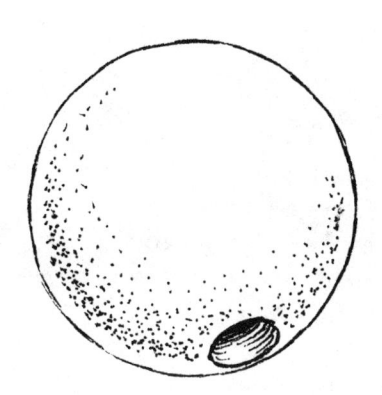

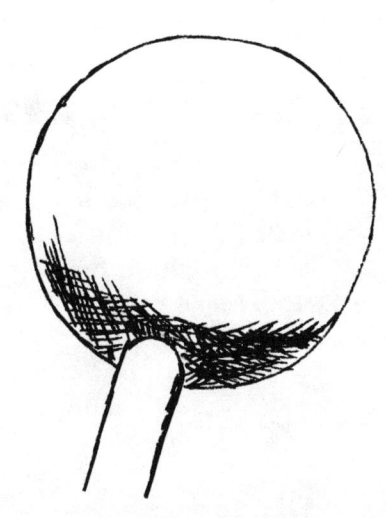

5. Glue the tube into the hole in the ball and cut the tube to the length of your forefinger.

6. Glue the head and neck into the hole in the top of your box.

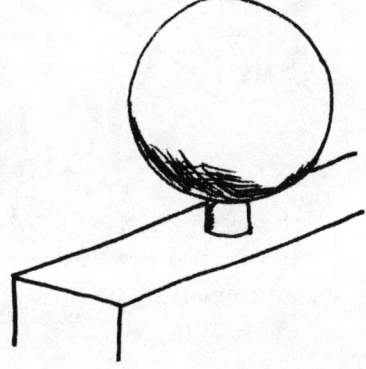

7. Cut two quarter-sized holes in the front of your box, make these the right size to fit the child's hand.

8. Next, cover the box with a bright material and glue a piece of felt on the side. Make lines on it for the pages.

9. Write or make the letters **BOOKER** in front of the box, and again in smaller letters on the side.

Booker's Bad Dream

10. Add felt or plastic eyes to the head of your booker.

11. Include some felt eyebrows and a felt mouth.

12. Glue on some yarn hair.

Booker Is Back

WHERE: In the library. WHEN: The present. PUPPETEERS: One. TIME: 8 minutes.

CHARACTERS

LIBRARIAN . . . . Librarian _____, head of the _____ Library
(Names of the librarian and library can be used)
BOOKWORM. . . . . A bookworm full of knowledge
BOBBY . . . . Optional — Bobby's voice can be offstage; or, Bobby, a puppet, can be on top of the stage or to one side and the area is lighted as he talks; or, Bobby can be a real boy.

At Rise: Bookworm is center stage crying. On the back curtain there can be a few felt or cloth books to look like a library shelf. Just the back of the books with title and author will do.

(The librarian stands in front of the stage but a little to one side.)

LIBRARIAN: Why are you crying, Bookworm?

(BOOKWORM sobs.)

LIBRARIAN: *(Moves a little closer to BOOKWORM.)* What in the world is the matter?

(BOOKWORM cries harder.)

LIBRARIAN: There must be something terribly wrong. What is it?

(BOOKWORM wails.)

LIBRARIAN: Please tell me what's wrong.

(BOOKWORM cries.)

LIBRARIAN: Do you have a problem?

(BOOKWORM nods her head yes.)

LIBRARIAN: What is it?

(BOOKWORM cries very loud.)

LIBRARIAN: Tell me about it. Maybe I can help.

(BOOKWORM continues crying.)

LIBRARIAN: Did you get the card catalogue mixed up?

BOOKWORM: *(Shakes her head.)* No.

LIBRARIAN: Did you put a book back in the wrong place on the shelf?

BOOKWORM: *(Shakes her head.)* No.

LIBRARIAN: Did you miss the children when they came to the library yesterday?

BOOKWORM: *(Shakes her head.)* No, no, no.

LIBRARIAN: Then what is wrong?

BOOKWORM: B-B-B-B-B-----. *(Cries.)*

LIBRARIAN: Yes, Bookworm?

BOOKWORM: Booker is gone! *(Cries hard.)*

LIBRARIAN: Bookworm, stop crying. I don't understand. Booker is gone?

BOOKWORM: Booker never came back.

LIBRARIAN: Where did he go?

BOOKWORM: Booker is lost. He is lost and gone forever. *(Cries.)*

LIBRARIAN: You mean somebody took Booker out of the library and hasn't returned him?

BOOKWORM: That's what I mean.

LIBRARIAN: Dry your tears, Bookworm. I will go to the file and see who has Booker. *(Exits.)*

BOOKWORM: *(After following the LIBRARIAN to the end of the stage, peers around the side of the stage after her.)* Thank you, Librarian. I miss Booker so much.

LIBRARIAN: *(Enters.)* Well, I found who signed out Booker.

BOOKWORM: Who?

LIBRARIAN: Bobby No-Return.

BOOKWORM: Bobby No-Return? Oh! No! *(Sobs.)*

LIBRARIAN: Yes, I'm sorry to say, Bobby No-Return took Booker out on his library card.

BOOKWORM: What can we do? Bobby No-Return has lost so many books.

LIBRARIAN: I know. All we can do is telephone him and ask him to bring Booker back. I'll get the phone. *(Exits.)*

BOOKWORM: That's a good idea. *(Peers around the corner again waiting for the LIBRARIAN.)* Please hurry, Librarian. *(To himself.)* Oh I hope Booker's all right.

LIBRARIAN: *(Returns with a small phone.)* I've got the phone.

BOOKWORM: Good.

LIBRARIAN: *(Puts phone on stage.)* I know the number by heart. I have called Bobby No-Return so many times. I'll dial the phone and you talk.

BOOKWORM: O.K.

(LIBRARIAN dials the phone – optional: sound of telephone dialing and ringing.)

BOBBY NO-RETURN: Hello?

Booker Is Back

BOOKWORM: Hello, is this Bobby No-Return?
BOBBY: Yes, it is. Who are you?
BOOKWORM: I am Bookworm from the _____ Library.
BOBBY: What do you want?
BOOKWORM: I believe you checked out Booker from our library.
BOBBY: Yes, I did.
BOOKWORM: Booker is overdue. Will you please bring him back? We miss him very much.
BOBBY: I can't bring him back.
BOOKWORM: Why?
BOBBY: I don't know where he is.
BOOKWORM: You mean you lost him?
BOBBY: I didn't lose him. I just don't know where he is.
BOOKWORM: Booker is lost! *(Cries.)*
LIBRARIAN: Ask Bobby where he had Booker last.
BOOKWORM: Bobby? Where did you have Booker last?
BOBBY: In my bedroom.
LIBRARIAN: Ask Bobby to look under his bed for Booker. Maybe he's under there.
BOOKWORM: Bobby, will you look under your bed for Booker?
BOBBY: O.K. Hold on.
BOOKWORM: Bobby is going to look under his bed for Booker.
BOBBY: Bookworm? Booker is not under my bed.
BOOKWORM: Booker is not under Bobby's bed. He is lost! *(Cries.)*
LIBRARIAN: Stop crying, Bookworm. Ask Bobby to look in his closet for Booker. Maybe he's there.
BOOKWORM: Bobby?
BOBBY: Yes, Bookworm.
BOOKWORM: Please look in your closet and see if Booker is there.

A Marker puppet in another guise (see previous section, pages 4 and 10–13). All children love puppets, both to watch <u>and</u> to delight others with.

Bobby: Oh, all right.
Bookworm: Oh, I hope Bobby finds Booker.
Librarian: I hope he finds him, too.
Bobby: Hello, Bookworm?
Bookworm: Yes, Bobby. Did you find Booker?
Bobby: He wasn't in the closet.
Bookworm: Booker's lost for good! *(Cries very hard.)*
Librarian: Ask Bobby to look everywhere in his room for Booker.
Bookworm: Bobby?
Bobby: What now?
Bookworm: Please look everywhere in your room for Booker.
Bobby: Look, Bookworm, I'm busy. Booker will turn up sooner or later.
Bookworm: Oh, please, look around your room for Booker. Please!
Bobby: This is the last looking that I'm going to do, Bookworm.
Bookworm: Bobby is looking for Booker one last time. I pray he will find him.
Librarian: Bobby has lost so many other books.
Bookworm: I know! I know! *(Cries.)*
Bobby: Hello, Bookworm?
(Bookworm keeps crying.)
Bobby: Hello, Bookworm? What's all the noise?
(Bookworm keeps crying.)
Bobby: I'm going to hang up. No use talking to you.
Bookworm: Don't hang up, Bobby! I'm listening. I'll stop crying. Did you find Booker?
Bobby: Booker is not in my room. I'm going now. So, goodbye!
Bookworm: Bobby! Wait! I have thought of one more place to look.
Bobby: I said, no more looking.

BOOKWORM: Bobby! Please! One last time.
BOBBY: Oh, all right. But this is the very last time.
BOOKWORM: O.K., Bobby. Do you have a book shelf in your room?
BOBBY: Sure, I do.
BOOKWORM: Will you see if Booker got lost in with your other books?
BOBBY: Booker can't be there. Just my books are there.
BOOKWORM: He might have been put there by mistake.
BOBBY: Oh, all right. But if he isn't there, I'm not going to look anymore.
LIBRARIAN: I hope Bobby finds him. We would miss not having Booker in the library. The children would miss him so much, too.
BOOKWORM: I miss him so much already. *(Starts to cry.)*
BOBBY: Hello, Bookworm? I found Booker!
BOOKWORM: You did? Booker's found! Bobby has found Booker!
LIBRARIAN: How wonderful!
BOOKWORM: Will you bring Booker back to the library?
BOBBY: I'll bring him right away.
BOOKWORM: Oh, thank you, Bobby. Thank you so much.
LIBRARIAN: Tell him I thank him, too.
BOOKWORM: Our librarian thanks you, too.
BOBBY: No sweat.
BOOKWORM: Goodbye, Bobby.
BOBBY: Goodbye, Bookworm.
(LIBRARIAN hangs up the phone.)
BOOKWORM: Isn't that super? Booker will be back soon.
LIBRARIAN: We will be so glad to see him.
BOOKWORM: I'm so happy I could cry.
LIBRARIAN: Please don't cry, Bookworm. You have cried enough today.
BOOKWORM: I guess you're right. I cry easily. But, it is wonderful. Booker will be here soon.

LIBRARIAN: It surely is. Booker is back.
BOOKWORM: Booker is back.

Props: A telephone and a telephone for Bobby if he is seen.

Production Note: Bookworm puppet can be made like the pattern for Country Cousin in *Old MacDonald Has a Barn* play.

Note: This is a good play for Library Week or Book Week. This play was designed to promote good library habits.

Optional: Phone dialing and ringing sounds.

Old MacDonald Has a Barn

Where: On Old MacDonald's Farm. **When:** One summer's day. **Puppeteers:** Six puppeteers, or two puppeteers by having the animals appear and disappear. The number of puppeteers is optional. **Time:** 15 minutes.

Characters

Old MacDonald .. An old farmer
Bookworm. . . . . A library bookworm
Klutzie Bird . . . . . . A fast, clumsy bird
Chick Chick . . . . . . A chicken
Gobble Gobble . . . . A turkey
Hee Haw . . . . A donkey
Turtle . . . . A slow turtle
Baa Baa . . . . A little lamb
Tornado . . . . A black tornado with a red eye
Quack Quack . . . . . A duck
Moo Moo . . . . A cow
Oink Oink . . . . A pig
Country Cousins .. Worms made out of socks

At Rise: Old MacDonald's farm animals are across the stage. A big red barn is at stage right. The animals make their

Old MacDonald Has a Barn

own kinds of sounds like: MOO MOO, BAA BAA, CHICK CHICK, etc. Old MacDonald is center stage. He has a basket in his hands.

MacDonald: *(Throws food from basket.)* Meal time! Come and get it! Food for you, Moo Moo. You are a lovely cow, Moo Moo. You give me such sweet, fresh milk.

Moo Moo: MOOOOOOOO.

MacDonald: *(Throws food.)* Here is food for you, Hee Haw.

Hee Haw: Hee Haw. Hee Haw.

MacDonald: Thank you, Hee Haw, for helping me with the work around the farm, like pulling the heavy wagon for me.

Hee Haw: *(Nods his head.)* Hee! Haw!

MacDonald: All my farm animals take good care of me, and I take good care of my farm animals.

Oink Oink: OINK! OINK!

MacDonald: By my chinny chin chin. I almost forgot my little pig friend. Move over Hee Haw and Moo Moo. Let Oink Oink have some food, too.

(Animals *eat the food and make noises chewing and talking.*)

MacDonald: Phew! Such a hot day! Not a breath of air stirring. *(Puts basket down and wipes head.)* I believe we are in for a storm. Yes, we are! *(Points stage left.)*

(Animals *cry excitedly. Wind sound.*)

MacDonald: By my chinny chin chin! We are in for a wing ding.

(Wind sound.)

MacDonald: Listen to that wind!

(Wind sound.)

MacDonald: Rake up my spuds! It's a tornado! And it's heading our way.
(Animals cry.)
MacDonald: It's a real twister. It's big and black!
(Animals cry louder.)
MacDonald: It is a dark funnel with a red eye.
(Animals cry even louder.)
MacDonald: It's coming right at us!
(Wind sound is very loud.)
(Animals cry and hold their heads.)
MacDonald: No time to run to the barn. Everyone lie flat. Get down low!
(Animals lie on stage.)
MacDonald: Here comes the tornado!
(Tornado rushes in stage left. It flies around the stage.)
Oink Oink: That's some tornado!
MacDonald: Get down, Oink Oink. You don't want to be blown away.
Baa Baa: I'm afraid!
Moo Moo: Me, toooooo.
Animals: Me, too!
MacDonald: If we stay close to the ground, we will be all right.
(Wind sound is very loud.)
MacDonald: The tornado is heading back towards us!
(Animals raise their heads, cry, then lower their heads.)
(Tornado swoops down over the animals.)
(Animals cry harder.)
MacDonald: Almost got us that time. By my chinny chin chin! Here it comes again!
(Tornado swoops over animals again and heads for the barn.)
MacDonald: The tornado is going to hit my barn!
Oink Oink: Keep your head down, Farmer MacDonald.
(Tornado rocks the barn, and then knocks the barn over

with a crash. The barn sinks below the stage and out of sight. All is quiet.)

BAA BAA: It's gone! The tornado is gone!

HEE HAW: Is it safe to come out?

MACDONALD: *(Gets up and looks around.)* The tornado has gone.

QUACK QUACK: *(Points to barn.)* Look, Farmer MacDonald!

MACDONALD: I don't see anything.

CHICK CHICK: You don't see anything because nothing is there.

MACDONALD: What's not there?

ANIMALS: Your barn! Your big red barn!

MACDONALD: *(Looks where barn used to be center stage.)* My barn! My barn is gone! The tornado blew down my big red barn! Oh, my beautiful red barn is gone. *(Wails.)*

(ANIMALS cry.)

MACDONALD: Oh, why did the tornado blow down my barn? I have been a good farmer all these years. Why me? Why me? Oh, woe is me!

HEE HAW: Old MacDonald lost his barn.

OINK OINK: A fierce tornado blew it down.

MOO MOO: With a huff puff here — Moo Moo.

GOBBLE GOBBLE: And a huff puff there — Gobble Gobble.

CHICK CHICK: And a crash bang here.

QUACK QUACK: And a crash bang there.

BAA BAA: Poor Old MacDonald.

(ANIMALS join together in song.)

    Old MacDonald lost his barn, E-i-e-i-o
    A fierce tornado blew it down, E-i-e-i-o
    With a huff puff here, and a huff puff there.
    Here puff, there puff, everywhere puff puff,
    Old MacDonald lost his barn, E-i-e-i-o.

MACDONALD: *(Cries.)* Why did that tornado blow down my barn? Misery! Misery! Woe is me! My barn is gone. There

Farmer MacDonald and farmer-puppeteer.

Old MacDonald Has a Barn

is no barn for you, my animal friends. Oh, woe is me! *(Shakes his head.)* Why me? Why me? By my chinny chin chin, I can't take care of you animals any more.

(ANIMALS cry.)

MACDONALD: Go and see if Farmer Brown will take care of you. *(Looks offstage.)* I see his barn is still standing. The tornado didn't blow down his barn.

OINK OINK: But, we don't want to leave you.

HEE HAW: No, we don't.

BAA BAA: We like it here. We want to be with you.

CHICK CHICK: Yes, we do.

MOO MOO: And how!

GOBBLE GOBBLE: You are good to us, Farmer MacDonald.

MACDONALD: I don't want you to leave either, but what am I to do? I am a ruined man. Oh, woe is me!

ANIMALS: We don't want to go. *(Cry.)*

MACDONALD: Stop your bawling. Be off with you. I am too old, and I am too poor to rebuild my barn.

OINK OINK: We don't want to go.

MACDONALD: There's no use talking. My barn is gone and that's that. So start walking.

OINK OINK: But, we don't want to go — ever!

MACDONALD: Quit the stalling. I said, git! And, I mean git!

(ANIMALS exit.)

MACDONALD: Misery! Misery! My beautiful red barn is gone, poof, just like that. *(Pause.)* For the life of me, I don't understand why my barn was blown down.

TURTLE: *(Enter slowly, talks slowly.)* Toooo bad, Farmer MacDonald, that tornado blew down your big red barn.

MACDONALD: Tell me about it.

TURTLE: That was some tornado.

MACDONALD: I don't want to talk about it.

TURTLE: I will help you rebuild your barn.

MacDonald: You? Ha! A slow-poke turtle like you rebuild my barn?

Turtle: I may be slow, but I do good work—very good work.

MacDonald: I would be dead before you could rebuild my barn. You are turtle-slow. I don't need your kind of help.

Turtle: I feel sorry for you, Farmer MacDonald. *(Exits.)*

Klutzie: *(Flies in very fast and talks very fast.)* Oh! My! Such a disaster! Did the tornado blow down your big red barn?

MacDonald: You don't see it standing there, do you? Huh? Do you? Do you, you klutzie bird?

Klutzie: No, I don't. No, I don't.

MacDonald: So?

Klutzie: So, too bad! Too bad! *(Trips.)* Eeeek! I just tripped myself.

MacDonald: What a klutz! As if I didn't have troubles enough without a klutzie bird coming along to bother me.

Klutzie: *(Looks over the stage where the barn used to be.)* Cuckoo! Cuckoo! There is not much left of your barn. Not much left.

MacDonald: Oh, go fly away. Far, far away.

Klutzie: I could help you rebuild your barn, Farmer MacDonald.

MacDonald: A klutzie bird like you? Help me? That's funny. Leave me alone! Go bother somebody else.

Klutzie: I work fast.

MacDonald: Shoo out of here. Shoo! Shoo!

Klutzie: O.K. for you. Cuckoo! Cuckoo! *(Exits.)*

MacDonald: Misery! Misery! Oh, woe is me! What am I to do? Fate has dealt me a cruel hand. I am a beaten man.

Bookworm: *(Enters.)* You poor man. I see the tornado blew down your beautiful barn.

MacDonald: I know. I know.

Bookworm: Can I be of any help?

MacDonald: You? What can a small worm like you do? Tell me that.

Bookworm: I don't know what I can do, but there must be something. Maybe I could help rebuild your barn.

MacDonald: Nobody can help me, a miserable old farmer.

Bookworm: There must be something.

MacDonald: Well, there isn't. What are you doing here anyhow?

Bookworm: I am visiting my country cousins who live in your gardens.

MacDonald: Then go, visit your country cousins and leave me alone.

Bookworm: I had a lovely trip from the city to your farm. I live in the City Library. I am a bookworm. I read lots of books. I have even read books about building barns.

MacDonald: Shove off, Bookworm, before I put you on the end of a hook and go fishing with you.

Bookworm: Oh, you poor man. You are so very upset. That's why you are so mean.

MacDonald: Git, Bookworm. Git! Leave me be.

Bookworm: Poor man! Poor man! *(Exits.)*

MacDonald: One thing I know, I don't need help from a book-reading bookworm. *(Yawns.)* Oh, I am so tired. *(Stretches his arms.)* My bones ache. Such miserable luck. I know nothing will ever be right again. What I need is some sleep to forget it all. *(Falls asleep and snores.)*

Turtle: *(Enters, carrying a saw.)* Poor Farmer MacDonald. He's so tired. He's sleeping like a log.

Klutzie: *(Enters, carrying a hammer.)* Here I am! Here I am!

Turtle: Sh! Farmer MacDonald is asleep.

Klutzie: I can hear. I can see.

Turtle: I've got the saw.

Klutzie: I've got the hammer.

BOOKWORM: *(Enters, carrying a can of paint.)* I've got the paint.

TURTLE: Let's get to work. There is much to do.

BOOKWORM: I brought some helpers to help.

TURTLE: Who?

KLUTZIE: Yes, who? Who?

BOOKWORM: My country cousins, that's who. Here they come now.

COUNTRY COUSINS: *(Enter, carrying saws, hammers and paint cans.)* Hello! Hello!

TURTLE: Great! We need all the help we can get.

BOOKWORM: O.K. everyone. There's a lot to do. Let's get to work.

(Everyone starts to work.)

KLUTZIE: *(Trips over MacDonald.)* Eeek! I tripped over myself!

TURTLE: Stop that, Klutzie. You'll wake Farmer MacDonald.

KLUTZIE: No, I won't. He's sleeping like a log.

(MacDonald snores very loud.)

(Everyone hammers, saws and paints as the barn rises from under the stage. There is a lot of happy talking and chattering.)

TURTLE: The barn is rebuilt.

BOOKWORM: It's better than ever.

COUNTRY COUSINS: It is! It is!

KLUTZIE: *(Flies to top of the barn and sits.)* It's a beauty. It's a beauty! Eeek! I almost fell off the barn.

BOOKWORM: Go trip over Farmer MacDonald and wake him up.

KLUTZIE: O.K. O.K. *(Flies to Farmer MacDonald and trips over him.)* Oh! My! Oh! My!

MACDONALD: *(Sits up.)* WWWWhat was that?

KLUTZIE: It's me, Klutzie Bird, tripping over you.

MACDONALD: Why in tarnation would you do that?

Old MacDonald Has a Barn

KLUTZIE: Bookworm told me to.

MACDONALD: Bookworm?

BOOKWORM: We wanted to wake you up. We want to show you something important.

MACDONALD: I don't want to see anything.

KLUTZIE: But, it's important, very important.

MACDONALD: I don't care if it is important. I don't want to see it. *(Lays down again.)* I just want to go back to sleep. I am sleeping away my woes.

TURTLE: But, Farmer MacDonald!

MACDONALD: I said, go away and let me be. *(Snores again.)*

TURTLE: Wake up, Farmer MacDonald.

BOOKWORM: Wake up, Farmer MacDonald!

KLUTZIE: Wake up! Wake up!

COUNTRY COUSINS: Wake up! Wake up!

MACDONALD: For pity sakes! Can't you let a poor old miserable farmer sleep?

KLUTZIE: But, you are not a poor old miserable farmer anymore.

MACDONALD: And, why not? Tell me that. My barn is gone. Right?

BOOKWORM: No, it isn't.

TURTLE: No, it isn't, Farmer MacDonald.

COUNTRY COUSINS: No, it isn't.

KLUTZIE: No, it isn't! No, it isn't! *(Points to the barn.)* Look! Look!

MACDONALD: *(Looks and rubs his eyes.)* My barn! I can't believe my eyes. My barn is right where it used to be and better than ever! Why, it's even a new barn. Surely I must be dreaming.

BOOKWORM: You are not dreaming, Farmer MacDonald. Your barn is real.

KLUTZIE: It's real, Farmer MacDonald. It's really real.

ALL: We built a barn for you!

MacDonald: Why would you do that after I was so mean and cross?

Bookworm: We understood. You had a great loss.

MacDonald: It's a miracle. That's what it is, a doggone miracle.

Turtle: We are your friends.

Bookworm: Everyone needs friends.

MacDonald: That they do, especially in times of sorrow and hurt.

Turtle: And, you need a little faith.

Country Cousins: Right!

MacDonald: Right! Faith and friends. Thank you, each and every one, for building a barn for me. You have made me a happy man.

Bookworm: We were glad to do it.

(Everyone agrees.)

MacDonald: I am so happy I could dance a jig.

Klutzie: Why don't you?

MacDonald: Oh, I'm too old.

Klutzie: You're never too old. Look at me. *(Falls off the barn.)* Eeek!

(Animals appear.)

MacDonald: My animals have come back.

Oink Oink: We just had to come back, Farmer MacDonald.

Hee Haw: We missed you so much.

Moo Moo: Farmer Brown was good to us, but we had to come back. We missed you so. We will live without a barn.

MacDonald: But, I have a barn. Look!

Animals: Farmer MacDonald has a barn. *(Chatter.)*

MacDonald: Oink Oink, go get me my guitar.

Oink Oink: Sure will, Farmer MacDonald. *(Exits.)*

MacDonald: Thank you, everybody.

Everyone: That's O.K. It makes us happy too. *(Chatter.)*

Old MacDonald Has a Barn

(OINK OINK *enters with a guitar.*)

MACDONALD: I'm so happy! I feel like singing. Join with me, everybody.

(Audience can join in the singing.)

> Old MacDonald has a barn, E-i-e-i-o
> And his good friends built his barn, E-i-e-i-o
> With a saw saw here and a saw saw there,
> Here saw, there saw, everywhere saw saw
> Old MacDonald has a barn, E-i-e-i-o

(Repeat with a hammer hammer, a paint paint, and a love love.)

MACDONALD: Let's dance the country hoe-down.

(Puppets dance.)

Music: Country Hoe-Down *by the Boston Pops Orchestra, Arthur Fiedler conducting.)*

(Curtain closes.)

Props: Basket for food for animals; hammers (can be made out of cardboard and painted); saws; paint cans and brushes; guitar.

Production Notes: The children can make the Country Worm Cousins as mouth puppets from a sock by making a large mouth, adding eyes and yarn hair. These puppets cost very little and the children love them. (See pages 34–37.)

The Tornado can be a witch puppet dressed in black with one red eye. It can also be a piece of black material with a red eye that is attached to a wire.

Children can do a square dance after the play. Friendship cards can be made and exchanged.

A Country Cousin

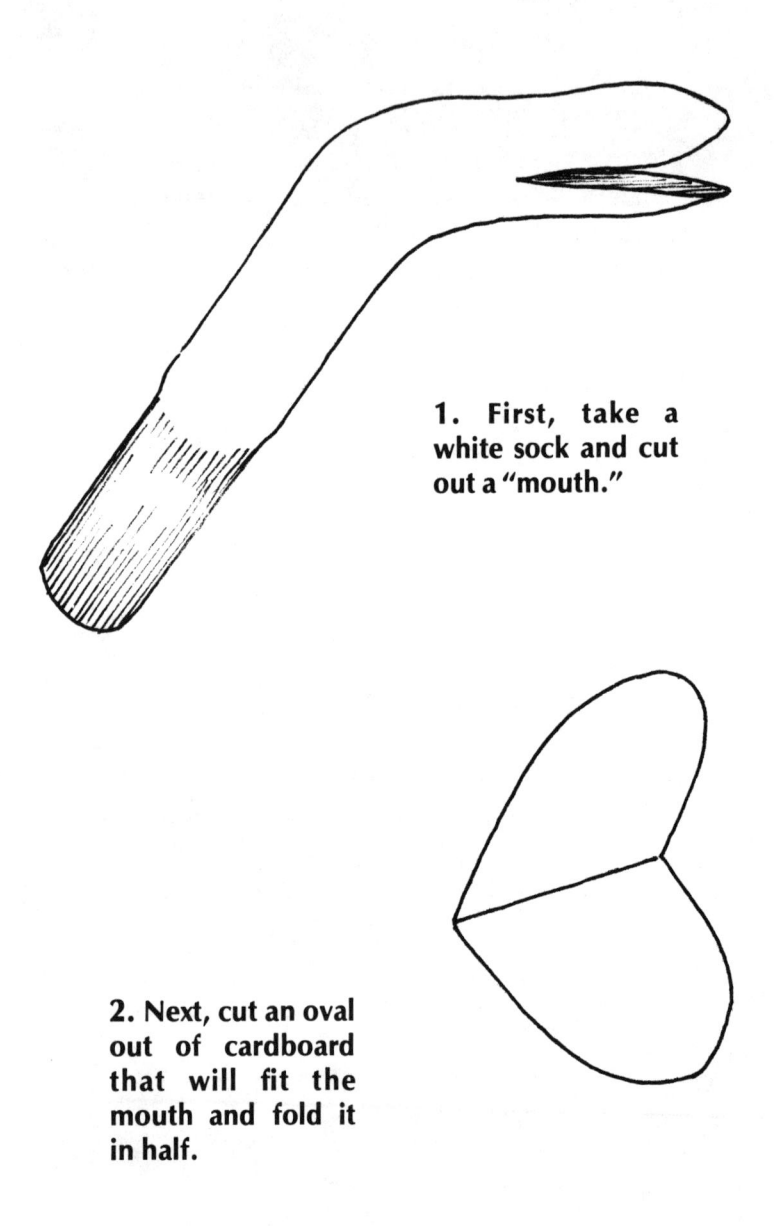

1. First, take a white sock and cut out a "mouth."

2. Next, cut an oval out of cardboard that will fit the mouth and fold it in half.

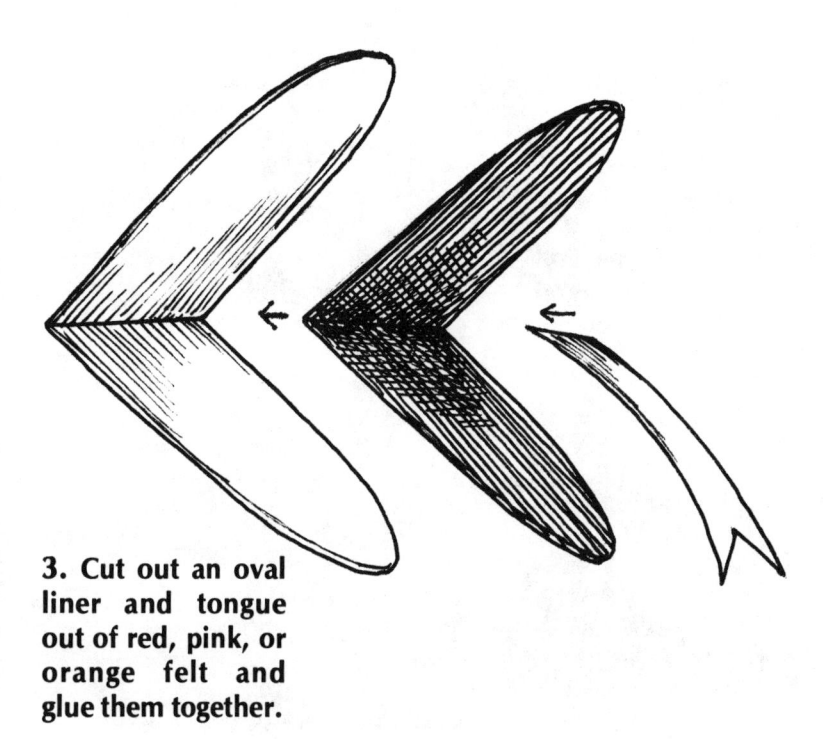

Old MacDonald Has a Barn

3. Cut out an oval liner and tongue out of red, pink, or orange felt and glue them together.

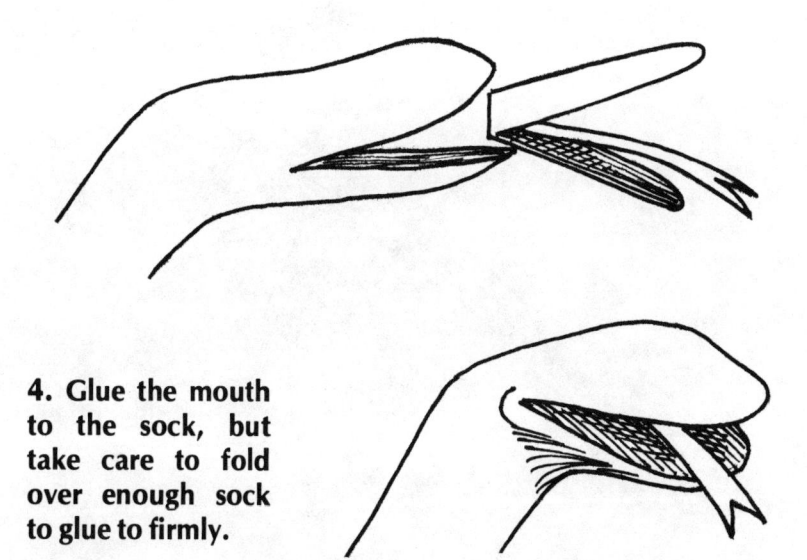

4. Glue the mouth to the sock, but take care to fold over enough sock to glue to firmly.

5. To make hair for your country worm cousin, first wrap colored yarn around a cardboard jig; the size of the jig will determine length.

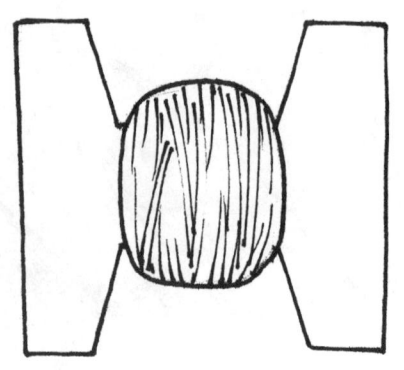

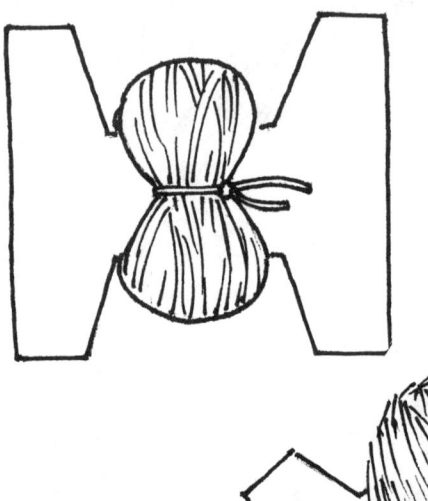

6. Tie one side of the yarn very tightly with another piece of yarn.

7. Cut the other side...

Old MacDonald Has a Barn 37

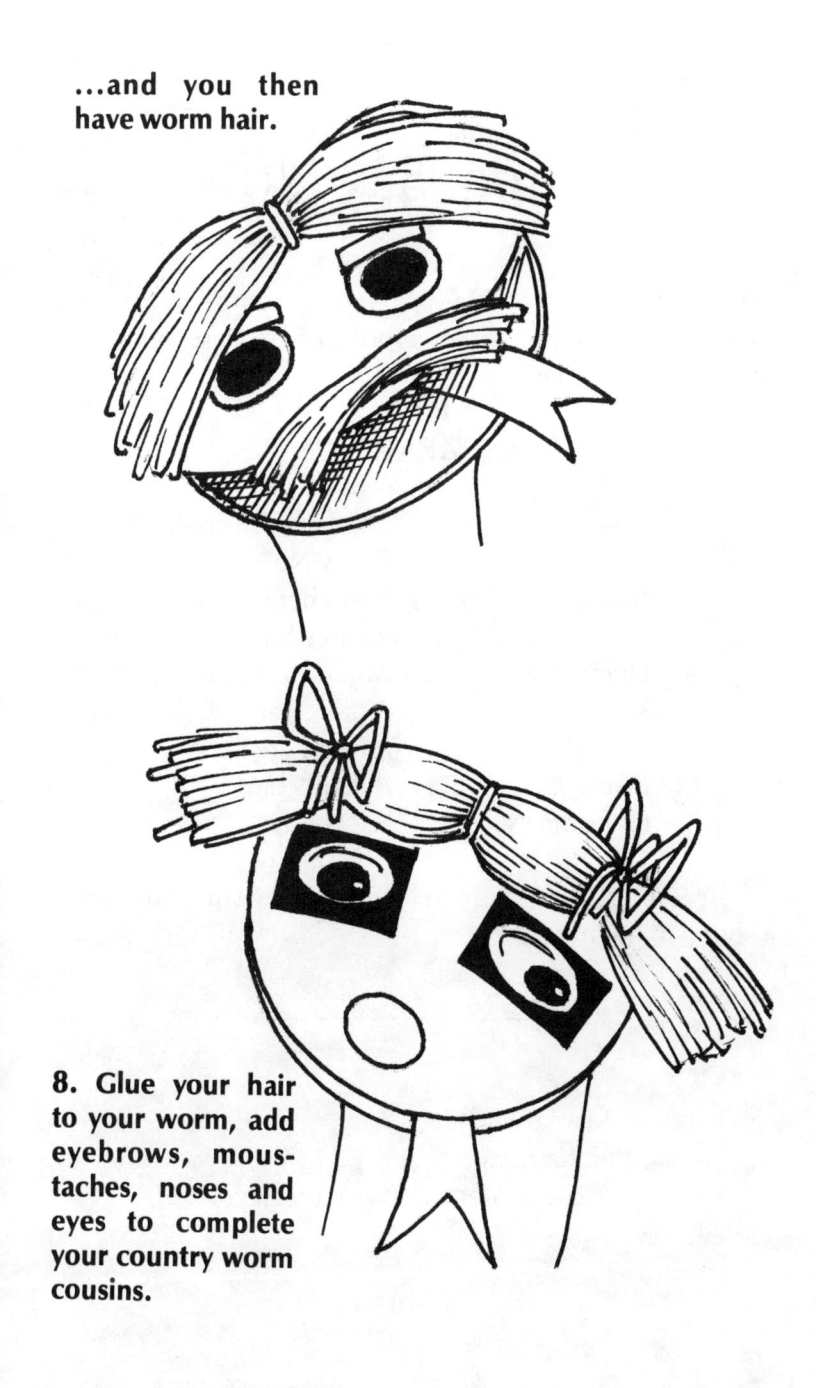

...and you then have worm hair.

8. Glue your hair to your worm, add eyebrows, moustaches, noses and eyes to complete your country worm cousins.

Papa, Say No!

WHERE: Papa & Mama's living room. WHEN: The present. PUPPETEERS: Three puppeteers, but seven can be used. TIME: 20 minutes.

CHARACTERS

PAPA . . . . A father who couldn't say "No"
MAMA . . . . A mother who loves to cook
RUDI . . . . A son who loves animals
UNCLE FRITZ . . . . An uncle who is a sponger
KATRINA . . . . A daughter who likes sweets
ALLIGATOR. . . . . A fierce creature
BIRDIE . . . . A flighty bird
LITTLE BUMPKIN. . . . . A fat baby

At Rise: Katrina is in the living room. Mama enters with a spoon in her hand.

KATRINA: Mama! Mama!
MAMA: Yes, Katrina?
KATRINA: *(Goes to Mama.)* May I have a cookie?

Papa, Say No!

MAMA: Not now, dear. I am making something special for dinner.

KATRINA: But, I want a cookie now!

MAMA: I know you do, dear.

KATRINA: But, Mama! Please!

MAMA: *(Shakes spoon.)* I said, NO, Katrina. *(Exits.)*

PAPA: *(Enters.)* Hello, my little Katrina.

KATRINA: *(Runs to Papa.)* Hello, Papa. Papa, may I have a cookie?

PAPA: I don't see why not.

KATRINA: Thank you, Papa. *(Exits.)*

RUDI: *(Enters.)* Hello, Papa.

PAPA: Hello, Rudi. What are you up to?

RUDI: Papa, I want to ask you a question.

PAPA: Ask away.

RUDI: Can I have a new pet?

PAPA: New pet? What's wrong with Bowser? Where is Bowser?

RUDI: Bowser's chasing a chipmunk. May I have a new pet?

PAPA: I guess so.

RUDI: Thanks, Papa. *(Exits.)*

(Katrina enters with a cookie.)

PAPA: *(Goes to Katrina.)* I see my sweet little girl has a cookie.

KATRINA: Yes, I have. Thanks, Papa.

(Doorbell rings.)

PAPA: There's the doorbell. I'll go. *(Exits.)*

(Katrina eats her cookie.)

MAMA: *(Enters with an egg beater in her hand.)* Who's at the door, Herman?

PAPA: *(Enters with baby.)* It was Mrs. Pickleheimer. She wants us to babysit Little Bumpkin.

MAMA: *(Throws her hands into the air.)* Honestly, Herman! Babysit today? Babysit when I'm so busy?

PAPA: Mrs. Pickleheimer wanted to do some shopping.
MAMA: *(Moves to Papa.)* But, Herman!
PAPA: I didn't have the heart to say "No."
MAMA: *(Shakes the egg beater.)* Oh, Herman!
PAPA: *(Holds out baby.)* Here, Mama, take this heavy baby.
MAMA: You took the baby. So you keep her. *(Exits.)*
PAPA: *(Walks with baby.)* I just didn't have the heart to say "No."
KATRINA: *(Goes to baby.)* Mrs. Pickleheimer has a heavy baby.
PAPA: Yes, Little Bumpkin is heavy. *(Holds out baby.)* Here, Katrina. You hold her.
KATRINA: *(Eats cookie.)* I'm sorry, I can't, Papa. I'm eating my cookie.
PAPA: *(Struggles with baby.)* Little Bumpkin is hurting my bad back. *(Puts baby on floor.)*
(LITTLE BUMPKIN *cries.*)
KATRINA: Little Bumpkin doesn't like it on the floor.
PAPA: I guess you are right. *(Picks up baby.)*
(LITTLE BUMPKIN *stops crying; doorbell rings.*)
PAPA: I'll go. *(Carrying baby, goes to the door.)*
MAMA: *(Enters with a rolling pin.)* Someone at the door again, Herman?
PAPA: *(Enters with baby.)* It was Mr. Knockinblocker.
MAMA: What did he want?
PAPA: He wants us to babysit Birdie.
MAMA: *(Lifts rolling pin over Papa's head.)* I suppose you said "Yes."
PAPA: Yes, I did.
MAMA: *(Starts to hit Papa with rolling pin.)* Oh, Herman! *(Decides not to hit Papa with rolling pin after all.)* How could you?
PAPA: *(Calls to Birdie.)* Here, Birdie. Come here, pretty Birdie.

Papa, Say No!

BIRDIE: *(Flies on stage. The tweets and sweets are pitched high. The cuckoo is pitched low.)* Tweet! Tweet! Sweet! Sweet! Cuckoo!

PAPA: Isn't Birdie a beautiful bird?

MAMA: You are the bird! *(Exits.)*

PAPA: I can't hold this baby another minute. *(Puts baby on floor.)*

(LITTLE BUMPKIN *cries.*)

BIRDIE: Tweet! Tweet! Sweet! Sweet! Cuckoo! *(Lays eggs.)*

KATRINA: *(Shouts over the noise.)* Papa! Mr. Knockinblocker's bird is laying eggs all over the place.

PAPA: *(Shouts.)* I can see that, Katrina.

KATRINA: Pick up the baby, Papa.

PAPA: Oh, all right! *(Picks up* LITTLE BUMPKIN.*)*

(LITTLE BUMPKIN *stops crying.*)

(BIRDIE *stops laying eggs.*)

PAPA: What a mess!

(Doorbell rings.)

PAPA: *(Is getting angry.)* What now?

KATRINA: Shall I go, Papa?

PAPA: No, I'll go. *(Exits with baby.)*

KATRINA: I wonder who it is? *(Eats cookie.)*

PAPA: *(Enters with baby.)* It's Uncle Fritz.

KATRINA: Is Uncle Fritz back again?

PAPA: I'm afraid so.

UNCLE FRITZ: *(Enters with suitcase.)* Here I am, you lucky people.

KATRINA: *(Hides cookie by turning away.)* How long are you going to stay this time, Uncle Fritz?

UNCLE FRITZ: Don't know. Had a miserable time. Cousin Jean couldn't cook worth a bean.

PAPA: Too bad!

UNCLE FRITZ: I'm hungry! I'm about to fade away. *(Sees Katrina's cookie.)*

"Papa," who learns to say "no," and puppeteer.

KATRINA: *(Backs away.)* You'll never fade away, Uncle Fritz.

UNCLE FRITZ: *(Reaches for cookie.)* Give me your cookie, Katrina.

KATRINA: I will not! *(Exits with cookie.)*

PAPA: Fritz! Take your suitcase to the guest room. You know where it is.

UNCLE FRITZ: That I do. *(Exits with suitcase.)*

PAPA: *(Walks with baby.)* How did I ever get myself in such a mess? First this heavy baby. Then that egg-laying bird, and now Uncle Fritz. *(Exits with baby.)*

(KATRINA enters eating a cupcake.)

UNCLE FRITZ: *(Enters and sees Katrina's cupcake.)* Ah! A cupcake!

KATRINA: *(Backs away.)* You can't have my cupcake, Uncle Fritz.

UNCLE FRITZ: *(Grabs cupcake.)* Yes, I can!

KATRINA: *(Chases Fritz.)* Give it back! Give it back!

PAPA: *(Enters with baby.)* What's all the commotion?

KATRINA: Uncle Fritz took my cupcake. *(Cries.)*

PAPA: Give Katrina her cupcake, Fritz.

UNCLE FRITZ: She can get another. Besides she's had two already. Maybe more.

PAPA: That is Katrina's cupcake.

UNCLE FRITZ: *(Gives cupcake to KATRINA.)* What a fuss over a little cupcake. I wouldn't say that was the proper way to treat a guest.

KATRINA: *(Stops crying and eats cupcake).* Hum! Good!

PAPA: What a day! *(Puts baby on floor.)*

(LITTLE BUMPKIN cries.)

(BIRDIE flies in and lays eggs.)

(UNCLE FRITZ grabs cupcake from KATRINA and exits.)

KATRINA: Uncle Fritz took my cupcake! *(Cries loudly.)*

PAPA: *(Shouts.)* Stop it! Stop it, I say! Quiet!!!

(Everyone is quiet.)

PAPA: That's better. Katrina, go find something else to eat.
KATRINA: Yes, Papa. *(Exits.)*
PAPA: Birdie! Go perch somewhere.
(BIRDIE *flies to top of stage.*)
PAPA: Wonder what will happen next?
KATRINA: *(Enters eating an ice cream cone.)*
UNCLE FRITZ: *(Grabs the cone from* KATRINA.*)* Man! Do I like ice cream cones!
KATRINA: *(Chases* FRITZ.*)* You can't have my ice cream cone. Give it back!
UNCLE FRITZ: You don't need anything more to eat.
KATRINA: *(Still chases* FRITZ.*)* Neither do you. I want my ice cream cone! *(Cries.)*
PAPA: Now, Katrina! Stop crying. *(Puts baby on floor.)*
(LITTLE BUMPKIN *cries.*)
BIRDIE: *(Flies in and lays eggs everywhere.)* Tweet! Tweet! Sweet! Sweet! Cuckoo!
MAMA: *(Enters wearing a hat and carrying a purse.)* I have had all I can take. I am leaving! I said, "I'm leaving!" Can anyone hear me? I'm leaving! *(Leaves.)*
KATRINA: Papa! Mama's leaving!
PAPA: *(Speaks over the noise.)* What, Katrina? I can't hear you.
KATRINA: *(Shouts over the noise.)* Mama's leaving!
PAPA: *(Shouts.)* QUIET!
(Everyone is quiet.)
PAPA: Now, Katrina, what did you say?
KATRINA: Mama is leaving.
PAPA: Where is Mama going?
KATRINA: I don't know, but she had on her best hat.
PAPA: Maybe she's gone shopping.
KATRINA: Not when she's making a special dinner.
PAPA: Maybe she needs something at the store.
KATRINA: But, she was wearing her best hat. I think Mama left us.

Papa: Mama leave us? Never!

Katrina: *(Holds her stomach.)* OOOOO! Papa! My stomach hurts. I think I am going to be sick.

Papa: You can't be sick. Mama isn't here.

Katrina: *(Doubles over.)* I can't help it. I feel awful!

Papa: I order you not to be sick.

Katrina: But, Papa! OOOOO! I want my Mama! *(Cries.)*

Papa: Don't we all. She will be back soon.

Katrina: Do you think so?

Papa: Of course I do. Go lie down, Katrina. It will make you feel better.

Katrina: All right, Papa. OOOOO! *(Exits holding her stomach.)*

(Mama screams offstage.)

Papa: *(Runs towards Mama's voice.)* That's Mama screaming. Mama! What's wrong?

Mama: *(Enters.)* It's Rudi!

Papa: *(Goes to Mama.)* What's the matter with Rudi? Is he hurt?

Mama: He's not hurt yet.

Papa: Then what made you scream?

Mama: *(Clasps her hands.)* You should see what Rudi's got.

Papa: Calm down, Mama, and tell me what Rudi's got.

Mama: I saw Rudi as I was leaving and... *(Puts hand to her mouth.)*

Papa: Go on, Mama.

Mama: You would never believe what he has roped. It's too horrible! *(Puts her hands to eyes.)*

Papa: What has Rudi roped, Mama?

Rudi: *(Enters pulling a long rope.)* I roped... *(Can keep pulling on the rope for suspense.)* ...an ALLIGATOR!

(Mama screams.)

(Papa yells.)

(Little Bumpkin cries.)

(BIRDIE *flies in and lays eggs.*)

RUDI: *(Shouts over the noise.)* Isn't he a beaut?

PAPA: *(Shouts over the noise.)* I can't hear you, Rudi. What did you say, Rudi?

RUDI: I said, isn't he a beaut?

MAMA: *(Waves her hands.)* Don't let that alligator loose, Rudi.

RUDI: I've got him tied, Mama.

PAPA: *(Looks at alligator.)* How did you tie him up like that?

RUDI: I roped him like a cowboy.

MAMA: You could have been eaten alive.

RUDI: I wasn't.

PAPA: Where did you find him?

RUDI: In our backyard. I can keep him, right?

MAMA: Wrong.

(ALLIGATOR *jerks the rope.*)

(MAMA *screams.*)

PAPA: *(Is holding the baby.)* Hold him, Rudi!

(ALLIGATOR *struggles and opens its mouth. Rope comes out of Rudi's hands.* ALLIGATOR *chases* RUDI.)

RUDI: The alligator's loose! Run for your lives!

MAMA: (ALLIGATOR *chases* MAMA.) We will be eaten alive!

PAPA: (ALLIGATOR *chases* PAPA.) We must capture him.

RUDI: How will we do that?

MAMA: I have an idea. *(Exits.)*

RUDI: Mama has an idea.

PAPA: I hope it is a good one.

(ALLIGATOR *does more chasing.*)

MAMA: *(Enters, carrying a blanket.)* Rudi, help me throw this blanket over the alligator.

RUDI: *(Helps with blanket.)* Smart idea, Mama.

PAPA: You used your head. You have the alligator captured.

MAMA: That will hold him until you can call the zoo.

RUDI: The zoo?
MAMA: The zoo keeper will come and get the alligator.
RUDI: But, Mama!
(ALLIGATOR *moves under blanket.*)
(MAMA *screams.*)
RUDI: But, Papa! You said I could have a new pet, and my new pet is that alligator.
PAPA: *(Shakes his head.)* Well, you can't have him, Rudi.
RUDI: But, Papa!
PAPA: *(Shakes his head.)* Rudi, I said, "No!"
MAMA: *(Shakes her head.)* Papa said, "No."
RUDI: Papa said, "No?"
PAPA: I said, "No."
RUDI: All right, Papa.
KATRINA: *(Enters, holding her stomach.)* Mama, I think I am going to be sick.
MAMA: *(Goes to* KATRINA.*)* Are you feeling ill, Katrina?
KATRINA: Yes, Mama.
MAMA: *(Feels* KATRINA's *head.)* You don't have a fever. Too many sweets, I bet. Come with me, Katrina. I'll give you some medicine. *(Exits.)*
KATRINA: Yes, Mama. *(Exits.)*
RUDI: *(Goes to* ALLIGATOR.*)* Do you think the alligator can crawl out from under the blanket.
PAPA: I don't think so. I'm going to call the zoo. You hold Little Bumpkin. *(Gives baby to* RUDI *and exits.)*
RUDI: Little Bumpkin? I'd say fat Bumpkin. *(Puts baby on floor.)*
(LITTLE BUMPKIN *cries.*)
(BIRDIE *flies in and lays eggs.*)
RUDI: Stop crying, baby! Stop crying, Little Bumpkin! Stop laying eggs, you dumb bird.
(LITTLE BUMPKIN *cries louder.*)
(BIRDIE *flies faster and lays more eggs.*)
RUDI: Papa! Papa! Come quick!

PAPA: *(Enters.)* Pick up the baby, Rudi.
RUDI: *(Shouts over the noise.)* Pick up the baby?
PAPA: *(Shouts.)* That's what I said.
RUDI: O.K., Papa. *(Picks up the baby.)*
(LITTLE BUMPKIN *stops crying.*)
(BIRDIE *stops laying eggs.*)
RUDI: You are smart, Papa.
PAPA: I learn. Good news. The zoo keeper will be right over. It's their alligator. It got out last night.
(ALLIGATOR *moves.*)
RUDI: I hate not having him for a pet.
PAPA: Bowser is a good pet.
RUDI: I know he is, Papa.
PAPA: Let's go and see if the zoo keeper is here yet. *(Exits.)*
RUDI: O.K., Papa. *(Exits with baby.)*
UNCLE FRITZ: *(Enters eating a big piece of cheese.)* Such a fuss over Katrina. What's a little upset stomach? I've had plenty of upset stomachs in my time. *(Pats his stomach.)* My! My!
UNCLE FRITZ: *(Goes to couch.)* The folks must have just had a new couch delivered. It looks mighty comfortable. *(Pats couch.)*
(ALLIGATOR *moves.*)
UNCLE FRITZ: That's funny. I thought the couch moved. *(Touches couch again.)*
(ALLIGATOR *moves.*)
UNCLE FRITZ: The couch did move! What a strange couch. Must be one of those vibrating couches. It would be a nice place to take a nap. *(Lays his head on couch.)*
(ALLIGATOR *pokes its head out from under the blanket and opens its mouth.*)
UNCLE FRITZ: *(Yells and throws the cheese at the* ALLIGATOR.*)* An alligator!
(ALLIGATOR *chases* FRITZ.)
UNCLE FRITZ: That alligator means to tear me to pieces.

(ALLIGATOR chases FRITZ.)

BIRDIE: Tweet! Tweet! Sweet! Sweet! Cuckoo! Cuckoo! *(Lays eggs.)*

PAPA: *(Enters.)* Bless me! The alligator is chasing Fritz.

UNCLE FRITZ: Help me, Herman! Do something.

(ALLIGATOR chases FRITZ.)

PAPA: *(Points to door, stage right.)* Fritz! Run out the front door.

UNCLE FRITZ: Why?

PAPA: The alligator will follow you. That will get him outside.

UNCLE FRITZ: What then?

PAPA: Then you run in the back door. I'll slam the back door before the alligator can get in again.

UNCLE FRITZ: O.K., Herman. Hope it works. *(Exits front door, stage right.)*

(ALLIGATOR exits front door.)

PAPA: I'll go to the back door. *(Exits back door, stage left.)*

UNCLE FRITZ: *(Runs in back door and runs across the stage. ALLIGATOR runs in back door and follows FRITZ.)* You missed, Herman!

PAPA: *(Comes in back door, stage left.)* I'm sorry, Fritz. The alligator was too fast for me. Try it again.

UNCLE FRITZ: *(Huffs and puffs.)* O.K., Herman. Get it right this time. I can never make it around again. *(Exits front door, stage right.)*

(ALLIGATOR exits front door.)

PAPA: I will shut the back door this time before the alligator gets inside. *(Exits back door.)*

UNCLE FRITZ: *(Enters back door and drops to floor.)* I can't run anymore.

PAPA: *(Enters back door.)* It's all right. You are safe, Fritz.

UNCLE FRITZ: *(Lifts head.)* Why am I safe?

PAPA: Because the zoo keeper has the alligator.

UNCLE FRITZ: You mean I'm not going to be eaten alive?

PAPA: That's what I mean, Fritz.

UNCLE FRITZ: *(Gets up.)* Well! Never in my life have I been treated in such a manner. Here I am a guest in your house. It is outrageous! I'm leaving!

KATRINA: *(Enters with suitcase.)* Here's your suitcase, Uncle Fritz.

UNCLE FRITZ: *(Takes suitcase.)* You recovered fast.

KATRINA: Mama gave me some good medicine.

MAMA: *(Enters.)* Sorry you are leaving, Fritz. You will miss my special dinner.

UNCLE FRITZ: Well, maybe I'll stay for your special dinner.

PAPA: Uncle Fritz is leaving now.

UNCLE FRITZ: No, I'm staying for dinner.

PAPA: No, Fritz, you are not. Go to Aunt Goody's, or somewhere else.

UNCLE FRITZ: I'll just do that! This is a nutty house. Don't expect me back soon. *(Walks to front door.)*

KATRINA: *(Waves.)* Goodbye, Uncle Fritz.

RUDI: *(Enters with baby.)* Have a good trip.

MAMA: Sorry you have to leave.

UNCLE FRITZ: It'll be a frosty Friday before I'm back. *(Exits.)*

PAPA: *(Takes baby from* RUDI.*)* Mama! I am taking Mrs. Pickleheimer's baby home now.

MAMA: You are, Herman?

PAPA: Yes, I am. And, I am taking Mr. Knockinblocker's bird home at the same time.

MAMA: You are?

PAPA: Yes, I am. Come Birdie. *(Whistles.)*

BIRDIE: *(Flies to* PAPA.*)* Tweet! Tweet! Sweet! Sweet! Cuckoo!

PAPA: Follow me, Birdie. *(Exits.)*

BIRDIE: Tweet! Tweet! Sweet! Sweet! Cuckoo! *(Exits.)*

MAMA: Isn't this peaceful?

KATRINA: It is nice. I'm hungry.

RUDI: Me, too. I'll go and find Bowser and tell him it's time to eat. *(Exits.)*
PAPA: *(Enters.)* This is more like it. Mama, I'm ready for your special dinner. I have worked up quite an appetite.
MAMA: Everything is ready. Just have to set the table.
KATRINA: I'll set the table, Mama. *(Exits.)*
MAMA: Thank you, Katrina.
PAPA: *(Hugs MAMA.)* I'm so glad you made us a special dinner, Mama, dear.
MAMA: And I am so glad you have learned to say no, Papa, dear.

Props: Cookie; cupcake; ice cream cone; piece of cheese; doorbell; spoon; rolling pin; egg beater; plastic eggs; suitcase; blanket; rope; hat; purse.

Music: Any German polkas could be used before and after the play, such as "Sing and Dance with Man Herzog" (Sound Records), Original "Böhmische Blasmusik" (Fiesta Records), "Singender Klingender Böhmerland" (Fiesta Records).

Production Notes: Children can make alligator mouth puppet from a sock.
Passing the baby from one puppet to another is difficult and needs practice. The baby can go for a nap to make it easier. Picking up the suitcase is also difficult and needs practice. A line can be added about sending Uncle Fritz's suitcase later. *Example:* UNCLE FRITZ: I'll send for my suitcase when I know where I'll be.
Children can dance the polka after the play.

Alligator Puppet

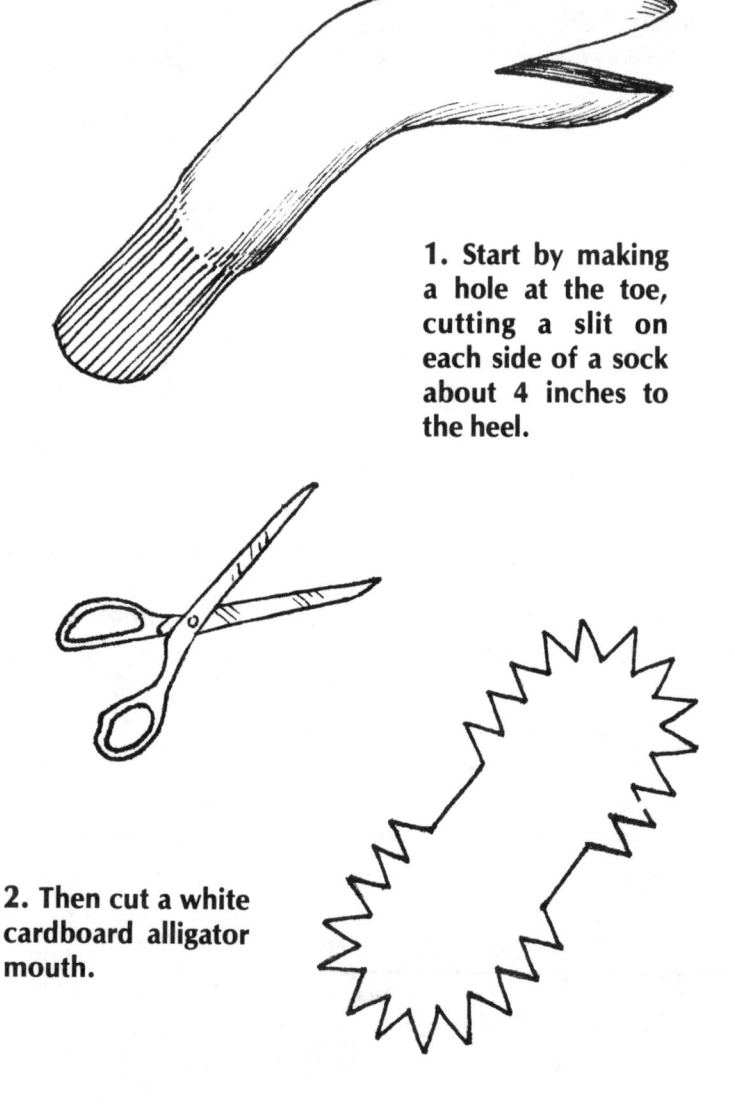

1. Start by making a hole at the toe, cutting a slit on each side of a sock about 4 inches to the heel.

2. Then cut a white cardboard alligator mouth.

Papa, Say No!

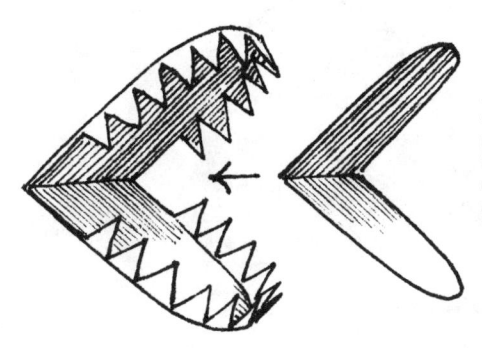

3. Fold the mouth in half and glue in an orange mouth liner (left).

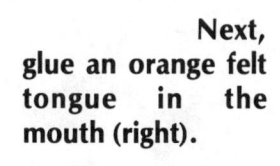

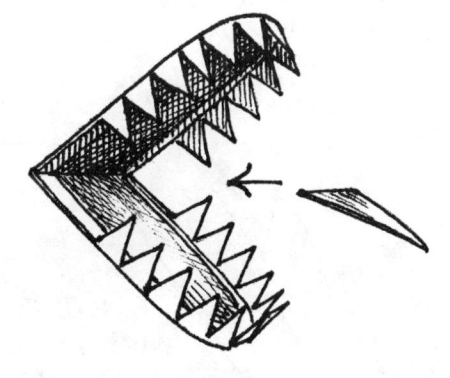

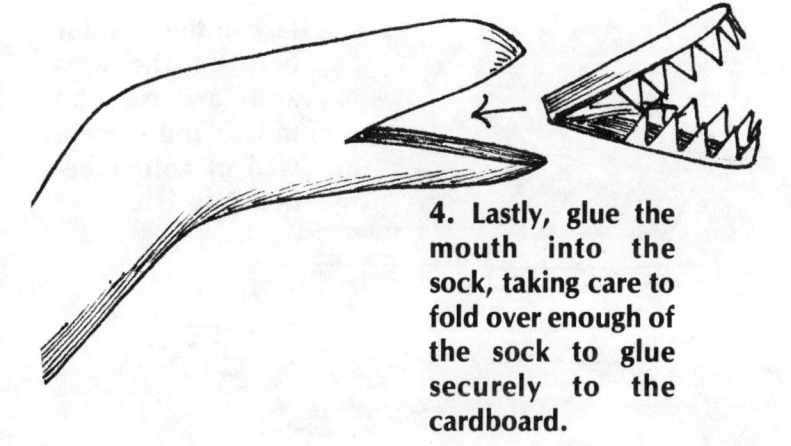

Next, glue an orange felt tongue in the mouth (right).

4. Lastly, glue the mouth into the sock, taking care to fold over enough of the sock to glue securely to the cardboard.

5. Cut a green felt oval about 6 inches long by 3 inches wide. Also, cut a strip 3 inches long and 1 inch wide with triangle cuts in the top.

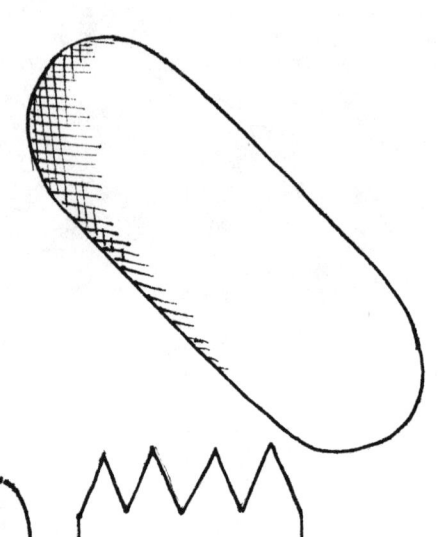

6. Fold the oval in half and staple the strip to it.

7. Staple some creases into the face of the alligator between the eyes and around the mouth and place a wad of cotton beneath the felt.

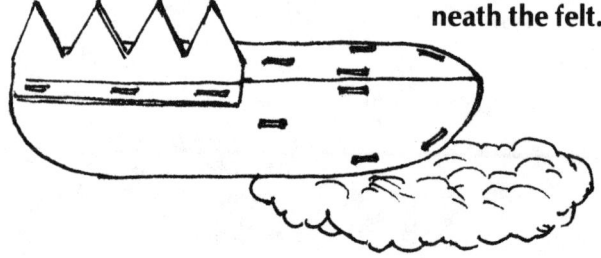

Papa, Say No! 55

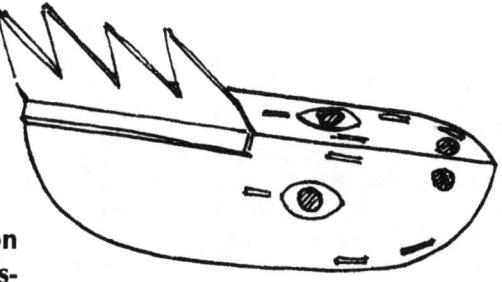

8. Next, glue on the eyes and nostrils.

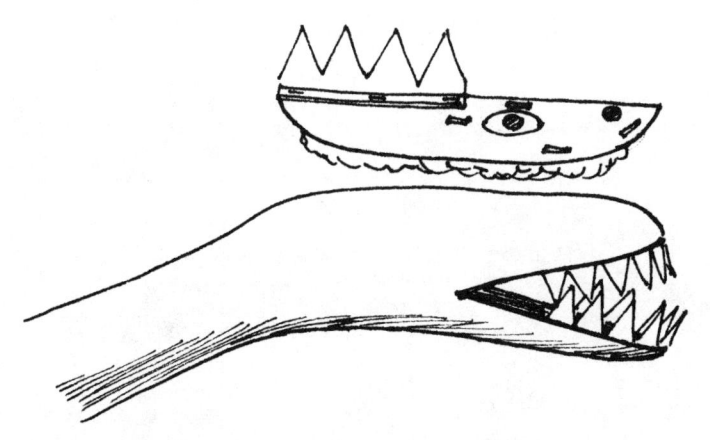

9. The last step is to staple the alligator skin to the sock and poof! You have an alligator puppet.

The Pillhilly Pig

WHERE: Pillhilly Mountain. WHEN: The present. PUPPETEERS: Two. TIME: 10 minutes.

CHARACTERS

PILLY PIG	A pig who thinks he's no good
SMELLY BOB	A skunk who can take care of himself
HARRY HATFIELD	A Hatfield who likes to fight a McCoy
MIKE MCCOY	A McCoy who likes to fight a Hatfield
MCCOY ANNOUNCER	A boy or girl
HATFIELD ANNOUNCER	A boy or girl

At Rise: The McCoy house is on one side of the stage and the Hatfield house is on the other. A rope is lying on the stage with the end of the rope offstage. Pilly Pig is center stage.

The audience is divided in half. One side will be for the McCoys and the other half is for the Hatfields. They are led by announcers.

The Pillhilly Pig

PILLY PIG: *(Walks back and forth.)* Oink! Oink! I'm nuthin' but a no-good Pillhilly Pig. Oink! Oink! Whatever I do, I fall into mud. Slop! Slop! I'm a pitiful porker. *(Shakes his head.)*

HARRY HATFIELD: *(Enters from behind Hatfield house.)* Wow! A pink pig! I've always wanted a pink pig fur a pet. Here pig! Here pig! *(Calls* PILLY *with a pig call.)*

PILLY PIG: That hillbilly can't be callin' me. I'm a no-good pig. Who wants a no-good pig like me? *(Shakes his head.)*

HARRY HATFIELD: *(Pulls* PILLY *to his house.)* Come home with me, pig. I want ya fur a pet.

PILLY PIG: Oink! Oink! *(Squeals.)*

HARRY HATFIELD: I'm goin' to call you Pinky Pig.

PILLY PIG: My name's Pilly Pig. I'm a Pillhilly Pig.

HARRY HATFIELD: O.K., Pinky Pig. You're my pet pig. Let's do some tricks. *(Raises his hand.)* First—sit up!

*(*PILLY *tries to sit up.)*

HARRY HATFIELD: Ya don't sit up good, Pinky Pig.

PILLY PIG: *(Sighs.)* I know. I don't do nuthin' good.

HARRY HATFIELD: *(Swings his arm around.)* O.K., Pinky Pig. Roll over!

*(*PILLY *tries to roll over.)*

HARRY HATFIELD: Pinky Pig! Ya don't roll over like a pet should roll over.

PILLY PIG: I know.

HARRY HATFIELD: Now, Pinky Pig, play dead.

PILLY PIG: I can play dead real good. I don't care if I'm dead or alive because I'm a good-for-nuthin' pig. *(Lies down.)*

HARRY HATFIELD: I've a lot of trainin' to do to make ya a good pet.

PILLY PIG: *(Gets up and sighs.)* I know.

MIKE MCCOY: *(Enters from behind McCoy's house.)* That Hank Hatfield's got himself a pink pig. That pink pig would make dandy pork chops.

HARRY HATFIELD: We're goin' fur a walk, Pinky Pig. *(Walks with* PILLY.*)* Stay at my heel like a good pet would do, ya hear?

PILLY PIG: Oink! Oink! I hear ya.

HARRY HATFIELD: You're not walking like a well-trained pet would walk, Pinky Pig.

PILLY PIG: I know! I know! I'm a no-good pig. I warned ya.

*(*MIKE MCCOY *sneaks nearer to* PILLY.*)*

HARRY HATFIELD: Ya don't think much of yourself, do ya, Pinky Pig?

PILLY PIG: That's right. I don't

HARRY HATFIELD: Why don't ya think high on yourself?

PILLY PIG: I've got reasons.

HARRY HATFIELD: What are they?

*(*MIKE MCCOY *sneaks closer to* PILLY.*)*

PILLY PIG: Because I'm a no-good pig. Nobody likes me and I don't do nuthin' right. *(Shakes his head.)*

HARRY HATFIELD: How come?

PILLY PIG: I don't know.

HARRY HATFIELD: Well, anyhow, I want ya fur a pet.

MIKE MCCOY: *(Grabs* PILLY.*)* And, I want ya fur pork chops!

PILLY PIG: Oink! Oink! Oink! Oink! *(Squeals.)*

HARRY HATFIELD: *(Pulls at* PILLY.*)* Give me back my pig, Mike McCoy!

MIKE MCCOY: *(Pulls at* PILLY.*)* This here pig is my pig now, Harry Hatfield.

HARRY HATFIELD: *(Raises his hands.)* This calls fur a fightin' and a feudin', Mike McCoy.

MIKE MCCOY: *(Raises his hands.)* We'll be fussin' over this here hog, all right.

MCCOY ANNOUNCER: *(Asks his side.)* Who ya fur?

MCCOY AUDIENCE: *(Shouts.)* The McCoys!

HATFIELD ANNOUNCER: *(Asks his side.)* Who ya fur?

The Pillhilly Pig

HATFIELD AUDIENCE: *(Shouts.)* The Hatfields!
MIKE MCCOY: We'll settle this pig problem right now.
MCCOY ANNOUNCER: *(Asks his side.)* Who ya fur?
MCCOY AUDIENCE: The McCoys!
HATFIELD ANNOUNCER: *(Asks his side.)* Who ya fur?
HATFIELD AUDIENCE: The Hatfields!
MIKE MCCOY: *(Hits HARRY.)* Take that, Harry Hatfield.
HARRY HATFIELD: How about this one, Mike McCoy? *(Hits MIKE.)*
(HARRY and MIKE fight.)
(AUDIENCE shouts who they are for.)
MIKE MCCOY: Here's the blow that will do ya in. I'm takin' this porker home for pork chops. *(Knocks out HARRY. MIKE pulls PILLY to his house.)*
HARRY HATFIELD: *(Gets up, rubbing his head.)* That Mike McCoy stole my pet pig. He's not goin' to git away with that. I'm goin' fur my brothers. *(Exits behind Hatfield house.)*
(PILLY PIG wiggles.)
MIKE MCCOY: *(Picks up rope.)* Hold still, you porker. I'm goin' to tie ya with this here rope. There's plenty of rope to do the job. *(Pulls on the rope.)*
PILLY PIG: Don't tie me up, Mike McCoy.
MIKE MCCOY: *(Keeps pulling on the rope.)* I don't want ya to git away.
PILLY PIG: I don't want to be pork chops! *(Cries.)*
MIKE MCCOY: *(Keeps pulling the rope.)* Too bad, fur I love pork chops!
PILLY PIG: This is the saddest day of my life. But, what else can I expect from a no-good pig like me? *(Hides his head.)*
MIKE MCCOY: *(Puffs and is tired.)* I'm about at the end of the rope.
PILLY PIG: Please let me go! I am at the end of my rope.
MIKE MCCOY: *(Pulls on rope.)* Shut ya mouth, pig, before I make ya into bacon.

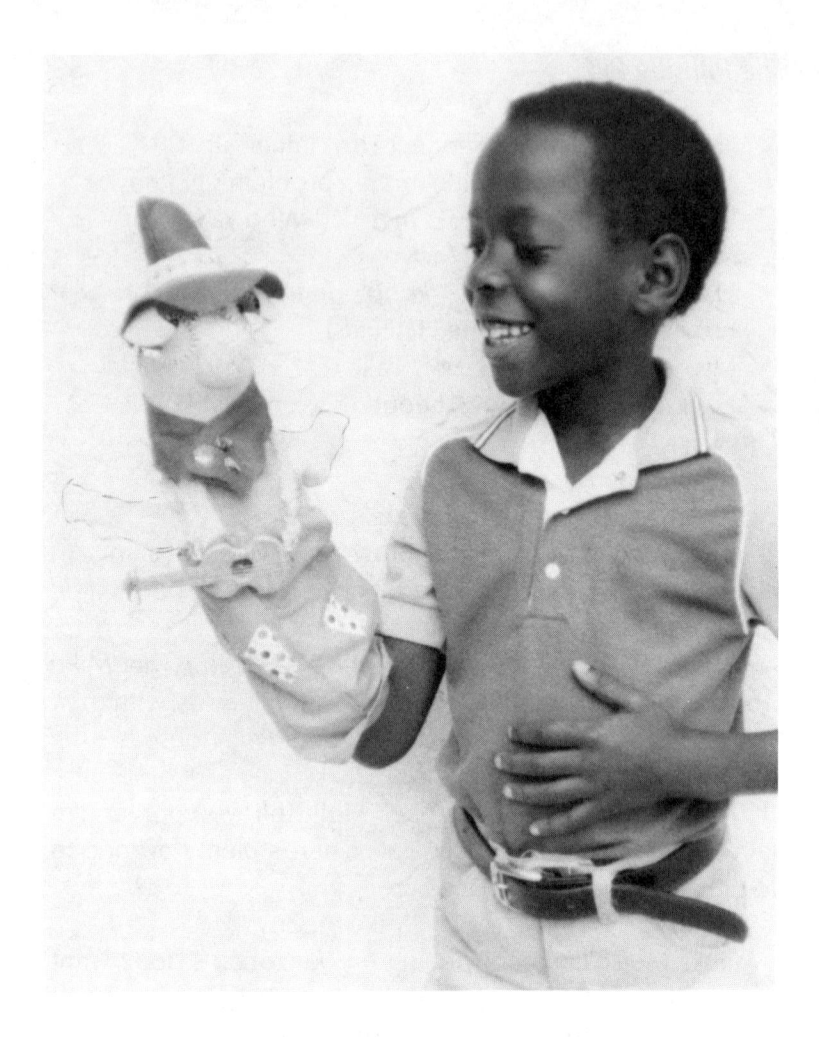

The Pillhilly Pig himself, and friend.

The Pillhilly Pig

SMELLY BOB: *(Enters, holding end of rope.)* What no-good hillbilly is pullin' on my rope?

MIKE McCOY: *(Drops rope.)* Smelly Bob!

PILLY PIG: Hello, Smelly Bob.

SMELLY BOB: Hello, Pilly Pig.

MIKE McCOY: *(Backs away.)* Git away from me, Smelly Bob!

SMELLY BOB: Then leave my rope alone.

MIKE McCOY: I need your rope. *(Picks up rope.)*

SMELLY BOB: What fur?

PILLY PIG: To tie me up so I can't get away. Mike McCoy wants to make me into pork chops.

SMELLY BOB: That ain't nice, Mike McCoy. *(Starts towards* MIKE.*)*

MIKE McCOY: I'm gittin' out of here! *(Runs behind McCoy house.)*

PILLY PIG: Ya made him run, Smelly Bob.

SMELLY BOB: I'm a stinker. What are you doing here, Pilly Pig?

PILLY PIG: I went for a walk and didn't look where I was goin', and the next thing I knew, Harry Hatfield had me fur a pet.

SMELLY BOB: Did ya like being his pet?

PILLY PIG: *(Shakes his head.)* Nope! Then, Mike McCoy wanted me for pork chops.

SMELLY BOB: I know ya didn't like that.

PILLY PIG: Then ya came along and rescued me. Thanks, Smelly Bob.

SMELLY BOB: Anytime. Ya better head fur home, Pilly Pig. 'Tain't safe near the Hatfields and the McCoys. They are always fightin' and feudin' over somethin'.

PILLY PIG: I'm goin' right home.

SMELLY BOB: See ya. *(Exits.)*

PILLY PIG: See ya, Smelly Bob. *(Starts to exit.)*

*(*HARRY *enters with his brothers.* HARRY *grabs* PILLY.*)*

PILLY PIG: Oink! Oink! Oink! Oink! *(Squeals.)*
HARRY HATFIELD: I've got ya, Pinky Pig.
MIKE McCOY: *(Enters from behind McCoy house.)* That Harry Hatfield has done brought his brothers. I'm going fur mine. *(Exits behind McCoy house.)*
HARRY HATFIELD: Thanks, brothers. We done scared away Mike McCoy.
MIKE McCOY: *(Enters from McCoy house with his brothers.)* Who scared Mike McCoy? It certainly wasn't a Hatfield.
HARRY HATFIELD: There's goin' to be the biggest fightin' and feudin' there ever was.
HATFIELD ANNOUNCER: Who ya fur?
HATFIELD AUDIENCE: The Hatfields!
MIKE McCOY: We McCoys will beat the hats off the Hatfields.
McCOY ANNOUNCER: Who ya fur?
McCOY AUDIENCE: The McCoys!
(McCoys fight the Hatfields.)
PILLY PIG: *(Sighs.)* Nobody's fur me.
(Fight continues.)
McCOY ANNOUNCER: Who ya fur?
McCOY AUDIENCE: The McCoys!
HATFIELD ANNOUNCER: Who ya fur?
HATFIELD AUDIENCE: The Hatfields!
PILLY PIG: *(Shouts.)* Hold it!
MIKE McCOY: *(Stops fighting.)* Who yelled "Hold it?"
HARRY HATFIELD: *(Stops fighting.)* Not me.
MIKE McCOY: Then git back to fightin'.
(Fight continues.)
HATFIELD ANNOUNCER: Who ya fur?
HATFIELD AUDIENCE: The Hatfields!
McCOY ANNOUNCER: Who ya fur?
McCOY AUDIENCE: The McCoys!
PILLY PIG: *(Shouts.)* I said HOLD IT!

The Pillhilly Pig

MIKE McCOY: *(Stops fighting.)* That no-good pig said, "Hold it?"

PILLY PIG: Yes, I did.

HARRY HATFIELD: *(Stops fighting.)* How dare ya?

PILLY PIG: I dared.

SMELLY BOB: *(Enters.)* That's tellin' 'em, Pilly Pig.

HARRY HATFIELD: Run or be shot at by Smelly Bob! *(HARRY and HATFIELD BROTHERS exit behind Hatfield house.)*

MIKE McCOY: We know when someone's stronger than we are! *(MIKE and McCOY BROTHERS exit behind McCoy house.)*

PILLY PIG: Ya sure git respect, Smelly Bob.

SMELLY BOB: That I do. So I see ya almost got captured again.

PILLY PIG: That I did.

SMELLY BOB: Glad to hear you ain't takin' any more hogwash.

PILLY PIG: It makes me feel real good, you know. I'm not such a bad pig.

SMELLY BOB: You're a fine pig.

PILLY PIG: I feel good about myself for the first time.

SMELLY BOB: What are ya goin' to do now?

PILLY PIG: *(Walks while talking.)* I don't know.

SMELLY BOB: *(Walks, too.)* Whatcha want to do?

PILLY PIG: I've always wanted to make somethin' of myself.

SMELLY BOB: What's been stoppin' ya?

PILLY PIG: Myself, I guess.

SMELLY BOB: Pilly, ya can be anythin' ya want to be.

PILLY PIG: I can?

SMELLY BOB: Ya can.

PILLY PIG: Can I be a doctor? *(Exits.)*

SMELLY BOB: Ya can be a doctor, if ya study hard.

PILLY PIG: *(Appears with a black bag with "DOCTOR" on it.)* I could be a famous doctor and make people well.

SMELLY BOB: Sure ya could, Pilly Pig.

PILLY PIG: I could be a lawyer or a judge. *(Disappears.)*

SMELLY BOB: Ya could be a lawyer or a judge.

PILLY PIG: *(Enters wearing a long, white curly wig.)* Here come da judge. Here come da judge!

SMELLY BOB: Ya'd make a grand judge.

PILLY PIG: I could even be a baseball player. *(Disappears.)*

SMELLY BOB: And play in the World Series.

PILLY PIG: *(Enters wearing a baseball cap with a "P" on it.)* I'd strike 'em out!

SMELLY BOB: That ya would, Pilly Pig. That ya would.

PILLY PIG: There is somethin' I want to be more than anythin'.

SMELLY BOB: What's that?

PILLY PIG: A country western singer.

SMELLY BOB: Then do it!

PILLY PIG: I'll do it!

SMELLY BOB: You'll have to work hard and see if ya have any talent.

PILLY PIG: I'll work like a hog. I'm off to Nashville, Tennessee. Thanks, Smelly Bob. *(Exits.)*

SMELLY BOB: Pilly's off to Nashville, Tennessee. *(Exits.)*

(Curtain closes. Hillbilly music can be played, such as "Mountain Dew" by the Stanley Brothers. Curtain opens.)

MIKE MCCOY: *(Enters from behind McCoy house.)* Are we fightin' and feudin' today?

HARRY HATFIELD: *(Enters from behind Hatfield house.)* There's more important things to do than fightin' and feudin' today.

MIKE MCCOY: Nuthin's more important than fightin'.

HARRY HATFIELD: This is. Did ya hear the news?

MIKE MCCOY: What news?

HARRY HATFIELD: My pet pig is comin' to town.

MIKE MCCOY: Ya mean my porker, Pilly Pig?

The Pillhilly Pig

HARRY HATFIELD: Yes, Pilly Pig is a big country western, super star pig now.

MIKE MCCOY: When's he comin'?

HARRY HATFIELD: He'll be comin' around Pillhilly Mountain any time.

MCCOY BROTHERS: *(Enter and sing.)* He'll be comin' 'round Pillhilly Mountain when he comes.

HATFIELD BROTHERS: *(Enter and sing.)* He'll be comin' 'round Pillhilly Mountain when he comes.

MIKE MCCOY: He'll be comin' 'round Pillhilly Mountain.

HARRY HATFIELD: He'll be comin' 'round Pillhilly Mountain.

ALL: He'll be comin' 'round Pillhilly Mountain when he comes.

(AUDIENCE *claps, led by* ANNOUNCERS.)

MCCOY BROTHERS: *(Clap their hands.)* He'll be wearing his pillhilly hat when he comes.

HATFIELD BROTHERS: *(Clap their hands.)* He'll be wearing his pillhilly hat when he comes.

MIKE MCCOY: He'll be wearing his pillhilly hat.

HARRY HATFIELD: He'll be wearing his pillhilly hat.

ALL: He'll be wearing his pillhilly hat when he comes.

(ALL *clap and sing.*)

    We'll all go out to meet
    Pilly Pig when he comes.
    We'll all go out to meet
    Pilly Pig when he comes.
    We'll all go out to meet
    Pilly Pig,
    We'll all go out to meet
    Pilly Pig,
    We'll all go out to meet
    Pilly Pig when he comes.

MIKE MCCOY: *(Points.)* Here comes Pilly Pig now!

PILLY PIG: *(Enters, wearing a cowboy hat with sequins, a*

scarf and dark glasses.) Eat your heart out, you Pillhilly people.

 HARRY HATFIELD: My pet pig is a VIP.
 MIKE MCCOY: My pork chops are famous.
 SMELLY BOB: What's a VIP?
 MIKE & HARRY: A very important pig!
 PILLY PIG: Right! Who ya fur?
 ALL: Pilly Pig!
 PILLY PIG: Who ya fur?
 ALL: Pilly Pig!
 PILLY PIG: Who's the best country western pig without a doubt?
 ALL: Pilly Pig!
 PILLY PIG: Shout it out!
 ALL: Pilly Pig!
 PILLY PIG: You bet your ham shanks I am!

 Props: A long rope; scarf, cowboy hat; doctor's bag (optional); dark glasses; sequin cowboy hat; judge's wig (optional); baseball cap with "P" (optional); guitar.

 Music: Boston Pops "Hoe-Down" by Arthur Fiedler, and "Mountain Dew" by the Stanley Brothers.

 Production Notes: This is a good play for audience participation. Many children can be in the play—six in the cast and as many Hatfield and McCoy brothers as desired. They can appear over the top and around the sides of the stage. The doctor, judge, and baseball player costumes are optional.
 The Pillhilly Pig was written with a hillbilly flavor. The correct English words can be substituted, or a deeper dialect can be used.

The Pillhilly Pig

The children made the Hatfield and McCoy brothers puppets.

Hillbilly music can be played before the show. Square dancing can be done after the play.

**See instructions for making the
Hatfield and McCoy puppets on pages 68-69.**

The Hatfields and the McCoys

1. First, using a dress pattern, cut out dresses, one color for the Hatfields and another for the McCoys. Then sew these together. Remember, you will turn them inside-out later.

2. Next, cut out some hands for them, using the glove pattern. Sew these to the dress and turn the whole outfit inside out.

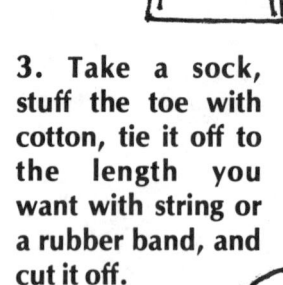

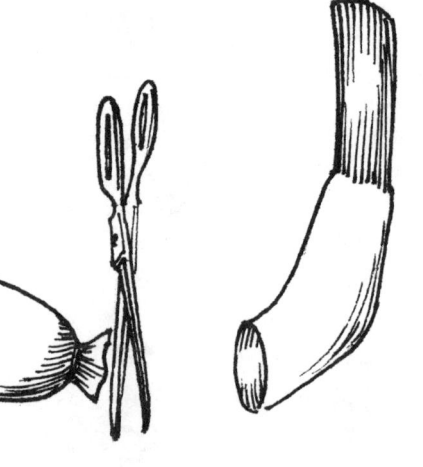

3. Take a sock, stuff the toe with cotton, tie it off to the length you want with string or a rubber band, and cut it off.

The Pillhilly Pig

4. Paint the sock tan, then glue felt face parts to it. Cotton or brillo pads can be used as beards.

5. Make a felt hillbilly hat and glue it to your hillbilly's head.

6. Finally, sew the head to the dress and glue patches to the dress and hat.

Your hillbilly is done!

Dusty's Flea Market

Where: Dusty Flea's living room. **When:** One morning. **Puppeteers:** Two, but five puppeteers can be used. **Time:** 15 minutes.

Characters

Dusty Flea	A boy flea who is a hero
Mother Flea	A mother flea who tries to keep her family together
Baby Flea	Dusty's baby sister
Dog Hounder	A mean, old villainous dog
Mrs. Flea Bargain	A lady flea who likes flea markets
Flea Shoppers	Mrs. Flea Bargain's flea friends
Sign Holder	Someone to hold signs

Music: "You Ain't Nothin' but a Hound Dog" can be played before play.

At Rise: Dusty is talking to Mother Flea. Dusty wears torn overalls and a faded shirt. Mother Flea wears a faded dress and a ragged apron. In the room there is an old table at one end and a broken chair at the other. Mother Flea is holding Baby Flea who is wrapped in an old blanket. Baby Flea is crying.

Dusty's Flea Market

The audience is told before the play by the SIGN HOLDER that signs will be held up at different times so the audience can take part in the play. Whatever the signs say, the audience does. For example: whenever the "APPLAUSE" sign is shown, the audience applauds. Or whenever the "BOO" sign appears, the audience boos. The SIGN HOLDER stands by an easel at one side of the stage throughout the play.

All the fleas speak in high, squeaky voices. Dog Hounder speaks in a low, deep, bass voice.

This play was designed for a group of children. Seven can be used in the cast, and any number for the flea shoppers.

Scene 1

MOTHER FLEA: *(Stands rocking* BABY FLEA *in her arms.)* Sh! Baby Flea. Don't cry.

DUSTY: I'm hungry, mother.

MOTHER FLEA: I know, Dusty, but there is nothing in the house to eat.

(BABY FLEA *cries.*)

DUSTY: *(Shivers.)* It is so cold in the house.

MOTHER FLEA: I know, dear. Dog Hounder has turned off the heat.

(BABY FLEA *cries.*)

MOTHER FLEA: I am hungry and cold, too. Oh, woe is me! We have come to this since your father went away.

DUSTY: What happened to Dad?

MOTHER FLEA: We have never heard from him since he jumped on a Redhound bus. Oh, woe is me! Dog Hounder is coming today for the rent.

DUSTY: But, we have no money to pay the rent.

MOTHER FLEA: Oh, dearie me! *(Cries and rocks* BABY FLEA.*)*
(Knock on door.)
MOTHER FLEA: That must be Dog Hounder now.
*(*DUSTY *goes to door exit.)*
DUSTY: *(Enters.)* It is Dog Hounder, mother.
MOTHER FLEA: Come in, Dog Hounder.
DOG HOUNDER: *(Enters, wearing a black suit, a black cape and a black top hat. He sports a black handlebar mustache.)* Goodday to you, Mother Flea.
*(*SIGN HOLDER *holds up a sign saying "*BOO.*")*
AUDIENCE: Boo!
*(*SIGN HOLDER *lowers sign.)*
DOG HOUNDER: *(Slouches and pulls his mustache.)* I have come for the rent.
*(*SIGN HOLDER *holds up sign saying "*BOO.*")*
AUDIENCE: Boo!
*(*SIGN HOLDER *lowers sign.)*
MOTHER FLEA: You know, Dog Hounder, I cannot pay the rent.
DOG HOUNDER: *(Slinks around the stage.)* But you must pay the rent.
MOTHER FLEA: But, I can't pay the rent!
DOG HOUNDER: The rent must be paid.
MOTHER FLEA: Not today. *(Coughs.)*
*(*BABY FLEA *sneezes.)*
DUSTY: Mother Flea and Baby Flea are catching cold since you cut off the heat.
DOG HOUNDER: You did not pay the rent. I will give you until tomorrow to pay the rent. If it is not paid — out you go! *(Points to exit.)* Grrrrr!
*(*SIGN HOLDER *holds up "*BOO*" sign.)*
AUDIENCE: Boo!
*(*SIGN HOLDER *lowers sign.)*
DOG HOUNDER: I'll be back tomorrow. *(Exits.)*

Dusty's Flea Market

(Curtain closes.)
(Music is played between scenes: "You Ain't Nothin' but a Hound Dog.")
(SIGN HOLDER holds up "NEXT DAY" sign. Sign is lowered.)

Scene 2

(Curtain opens.)
MOTHER FLEA: *(Coughs.)* I am chilled to the bone since Dog Hounder turned off the heat. I may be getting pneumonia.
(BABY FLEA sneezes.)
MOTHER FLEA: *(Hugs BABY FLEA.)* Poor little tyke. Baby Flea is so cold. She may get pneumonia. We may all get pneumonia.
(Knock on the door.)
MOTHER FLEA: That must be Dog Hounder. Go to the door, Dusty, please.
DUSTY: *(Goes to door exit.)* Yes mother. *(Enters.)* It is Dog Hounder. He is here for the rent.
DOG HOUNDER: *(Enters and slinks around.)* Grrrr!
(SIGN HOLDER holds up "BOO" sign.)
AUDIENCE: Boo!
(SIGN HOLDER lowers sign.)
DOG HOUNDER: Ah, good morning, Mother Flea. Isn't this is a beautiful morning?
MOTHER FLEA: I don't see anything beautiful about it. We are cold and hungry.
DUSTY: You know we don't have the money to pay the rent.
MOTHER FLEA: We are poor as church mice.
DOG HOUNDER: Don't poor-mouth me. You fleas give me the itch. The only decent one is Baby Flea. *(Goes to BABY FLEA.)* Goochy Goo!
(BABY FLEA cries.)

Dusty Flea and Dog Hounder, with delighted manipulator.

Dusty's Flea Market

Dusty: Baby Flea doesn't like you. I don't like you either.
(Sign Holder *holds up "boo" sign.*)
Audience: Boo!
(Sign Holder *lowers sign.*)
Mother Flea: Dog Hounder, I know you are here for the rent.
Dog Hounder: That I am, madam.
Mother Flea: You know I can't pay the rent.
Dog Hounder: You must pay the rent, or out you go.
(Sign Holder *holds up "boo" sign.*)
Audience: Boo!
(Sign Holder *lifts "boo" sign higher.*)
Audience: Boo!
(Sign Holder *lowers sign.*)
Dog Hounder: This may be a tear jerker, but the rent must be paid. Arf! Arf!
Dusty: Oh, go stick a burr to your tail.
(Sign Holder *holds up "applause" sign.*)
(Audience *claps.*)
(Sign Holder *lowers sign.*)
Dog Hounder: Look who's talking. *(Lifts his arm.)* I could flatten you with one whack.
(Sign Holder *holds up "boo" sign.*)
Audience: Boo!
(Sign Holder *lowers sign.*)
Mother Flea: Please, Dog Hounder. Do not hurt my son.
Dusty: I'll get the dog catcher after you.
(Sign Holder *holds up "applause" sign.*)
(Audience *claps.*)
(Sign Holder *lowers sign.*)
Dusty: You are a cruel, mean dog!
(Sign Holder *holds up "applause" sign.*)
(Audience *claps.*)
(Sign Holder *lowers sign.*)

DOG HOUNDER: *(Moves to* DUSTY.*)* Grrrr!

MOTHER FLEA: *(Is worried.)* Stop it, Dusty! Dog Hounder is upset.

DOG HOUNDER: *(Goes to* MOTHER FLEA.*)* You're doggone right I'm upset. Grrrr! This will teach you. *(Grabs* BABY FLEA.*)*

*(*BABY FLEA *cries.)*

MOTHER FLEA: My baby! My baby!

DOG HOUNDER: You will not get Baby Flea back until you pay the rent. *(Exits with* BABY FLEA.*)*

*(*SIGN HOLDER *holds up "*BOO*" sign.)*

AUDIENCE: Boo!

*(*SIGN HOLDER *lowers sign.)*

MOTHER FLEA: My baby! My baby!

DUSTY FLEA: Dog Hounder has fleanapped Baby Flea! There's a law against fleanapping.

MOTHER FLEA: I don't know what to do. *(Wails.)*

DUSTY: *(Raises his hand.)* I will get Baby Flea back!

*(*SIGN HOLDER *raises "*APPLAUSE*" sign.)*

*(*AUDIENCE *claps.)*

*(*SIGN HOLDER *lowers sign.)*

MOTHER FLEA: But, Dusty, how will you do that?

DUSTY: I haven't a clue, but I will find a way.

MOTHER FLEA: I don't think you can. What will I do? *(cries and exits.)*

DUSTY: I will save Baby Flea.

*(*SIGN HOLDER *holds up "*APPLAUSE*" sign.)*

*(*AUDIENCE *claps.)*

*(*SIGN HOLDER *lowers sign.)*

DUSTY: But, how? I need money. How will I get some money? *(Sighs.)*

(Knock on the door.)

DUSTY: *(Goes to door exit.)* Could that be Dog Hounder bringing Baby Flea home? *(Enters with* MRS. FLEA BARGAIN.*)* What did you say your name was?

MRS. FLEA BARGAIN: My name is Mrs. Flea Bargain.

Dusty: What can I do to help you, Mrs. Flea Bargain?

Mrs. Flea Bargain: I was passing this dump, I mean, this house, and I couldn't resist stopping.

Dusty: What did you stop for?

Mrs. Flea Bargain: I just knew that there might be some bargains in here. *(Rushes to the chair.)* Oh, mercy, that chair! It's the very chair I have been looking all over for. How much is it?

Dusty: But, that chair is broken.

Mrs. Flea Bargain: That doesn't matter. My husband will repair it. How much is it?

Dusty: A—A dollar?

Mrs. Flea Bargain: A dollar! What a bargain. Wait until the girls hear about this place. *(Gives Dusty a dollar.)* Here's your dollar, young man. What is the name of your flea market?

Dusty: My what?

Mrs. Flea Bargain: Your flea market. This is a flea market, isn't it?

Dusty: Oh, y-y-yes, it's a flea market, all right. I call it— Dusty's Flea Market.

(Lights go out.)

Dusty: Darn that Dog Hounder. Now he has turned off the lights.

Mrs. Flea Bargain: Why would Dog Hounder turn off your lights?

Dusty: Don't worry, Mrs. Flea Bargain. Don't move. I'll be right back. *(Gropes his way off stage.)*

Mrs. Flea Bargain: The girls will not like to shop in the dark. I don't like the dark. I don't like the dark one little bit.

Dusty: *(Flips small lights on a wire—Christmas tree lights that go on and off—from the back of the stage with a broomstick. Lights are pushed over from the back.)* Mrs. Flea Bargain! How do you like these? These Christmas lights run on batteries. They are better than lights.

MRS. FLEA BARGAIN: How ingenious of you. What a clever idea. The girls will like flea shopping with these twinkling lights. What else do you have to show me, young man?

DUSTY: I don't have anything now. Oh, but I will have some of the greatest bargains in the world to show you, real soon.

MRS. FLEA BARGAIN: Good. I will be back as soon as I spread the word to my flea friends. I'll pick up my chair with the other bargains later. *(Exits.)*

DUSTY: Goodbye, Mrs. Flea Bargain. And, thank you. *(Shakes his head.)* Doggone! How am I to find things to sell to Mrs. Flea Bargain and her friends? I don't know the first thing about a flea market. I know! I will look in trash cans, in the City Dump and in our attic. I will have the best flea market ever! *(Raises his hand.)* "Seek and ye shall find," Grandma Flea always said. *(Exits.)*

(Curtain closes.)

(Music is played between scenes: "You Ain't Nothin' but a Hound Dog.")

(SIGN HOLDER holds up "NEXT DAY" sign. Sign is lowered.)

Scene 3

(Curtain Opens. DUSTY is sorting things on bargain table, which is covered with many flea bargains.)

MOTHER FLEA: *(Enters.)* Dusty, I'm glad you found the Christmas lights since Dog Hounder turned off our lights. What are you doing with all that junk on the table?

DUSTY: This isn't junk. It's my flea market. *(Exits.)*

MOTHER FLEA: Dusty! Come back here! What are you talking about?

DUSTY: *(Pokes his head over top of stage. He flips a sign that says, "DUSTY'S FLEA MARKET.")* I am talking about the new DUSTY'S FLEA MARKET.

MOTHER FLEA: Have you gone flea happy? Baby Flea is gone; we have no food or heat; and Dog Hounder has turned off the lights.

DUSTY: I am going to get Baby Flea back!

(SIGN HOLDER *lifts up* "APPLAUSE" *sign.*)

(AUDIENCE *claps.*)

(SIGN HOLDER *lowers sign.*)

MOTHER FLEA: How can you get Baby Flea back?

DUSTY: The money I make from my flea market will pay the rent and we can get Baby Flea back.

MOTHER FLEA: Oh, Dusty! Do you think so?

DUSTY: Of course, I think so.

(Knock on the door.)

DUSTY: That must be Mrs. Flea Bargain and her friends. *(Runs to door exit.)*

MOTHER FLEA: I think I'm dreaming.

DUSTY: *(Takes* MRS. FLEA BARGAIN *and her friends to the bargain table.)* Right this way, Mrs. Flea Bargain.

MRS. FLEA BARGAIN: *(Buys something.)* See, girls! What did I tell you?

FLEA SHOPPERS: Oh, my! Such marvelous bargains! Look at this! *(And so on; they buy many things and give* DUSTY *paper money. This scene can be as big as you want to make it.)*

(Music played while the shoppers shop: "You Ain't Nothin' but a Hound Dog.")

MOTHER FLEA: I will help you, Dusty. *(Waits on the customers.)*

MRS. FLEA BARGAIN: Come on girls. We have bought enough today. *(Exits.)*

*(*FLEA SHOPPERS *exit, chattering about their bargains.)*

MOTHER FLEA: Look at all the money you made, Dusty. We can pay the rent and get Baby Flea back.

(SIGN HOLDER *holds up* "HOORAY" *sign.*)

AUDIENCE: Hooray!

(Lights come back on.)

MOTHER FLEA: The lights! They are on again.

DUSTY: Wonder how come?

MOTHER FLEA: Who knows when it comes to Dog Hounder.

(Knock on the door.)

DUSTY: More Customers? *(Runs to door exit.)*

MOTHER FLEA: But there is nothing left to sell.

DUSTY: *(Enters.)* You won't believe who's here.

MOTHER FLEA: Who is here?

DUSTY: It's Dog Hounder and he has Baby Flea!

DOG HOUNDER: *(Enters, carrying BABY FLEA.)* Take this Baby Flea back. I can't stand her. She gives me the itch.

MOTHER FLEA: My baby! My baby! Give me Baby Flea! *(Takes BABY FLEA.)*

DOG HOUNDER: With pleasure. *(Scratches himself.)* Oh, how I itch!

DUSTY: I'll fix that. *(Exits.)*

DOG HOUNDER: I decided to bring Baby Flea home and throw you out of the house instead. I turned on the lights so I can rent the house to someone else.

(SIGN HOLDER holds up "BOO" sign.)

AUDIENCE: Boo!

(SIGN HOLDER lowers sign.)

DUSTY: *(Enters.)* Here, this will fix your itch! *(Throws flea powder at Dog Hounder from a flea powder can. This scene can be as big as you wish to make it. A fun scene.)*

DOG HOUNDER: *(Sneezes.)* Curr-choo! Curr-choo!

(SIGN HOLDER holds up "APPLAUSE" sign.)

(AUDIENCE claps.)

(SIGN HOLDER lowers sign.)

DUSTY: You flea-bitten old hound. *(Gives DOG HOUNDER the money.)* Here is the money to pay the rent.

(SIGN HOLDER holds up "APPLAUSE" sign.)

(AUDIENCE claps.)

(SIGN HOLDER lowers sign.)

Dusty's Flea Market

DUSTY: I should exterminate you, you miserable dog.
(SIGN HOLDER *holds up "*HOORAY*" sign.*)
AUDIENCE: Hooray!
(SIGN HOLDER *lowers sign.*)
DUSTY: *(Points to exit.)* Get out of here!
DOG HOUNDER: Currrses! Flea marketed again. Guess I've been barking up the wrong tree. Think I'll go find a fire hydrant.
(SIGN HOLDER *holds up "*BOO*" sign.*)
AUDIENCE: Boo! Boo!
(DOG HOUNDER *exits.*)
MOTHER FLEA: I am so proud of you, Dusty.
DUSTY: I'm proud of me, too.
(SIGN HOLDER *holds up "*APPLAUSE*" sign.*)
(AUDIENCE *claps.*)
(*Curtain closes.*)
(*Music is played:* "You Ain't Nothin' but a Hound Dog.")

Props: Signs: DUSTY'S FLEA MARKET, BOO!, APPLAUSE, HOORAY!, NEXT DAY; flashlight; blinking lights; table; broom; flea powder can; paper money; chair.

Music: A good record to use is Elvis Presley's "You Ain't Nothin' but a Hound Dog."

Production Notes: A melodrama is a fun play to do. It is a play of good versus bad, and the good wins. Voice, gestures, emotions and actions are highly exaggerated.
Children can make things for the Flea Market and the Flea Shopper puppets.

A Flea Puppet

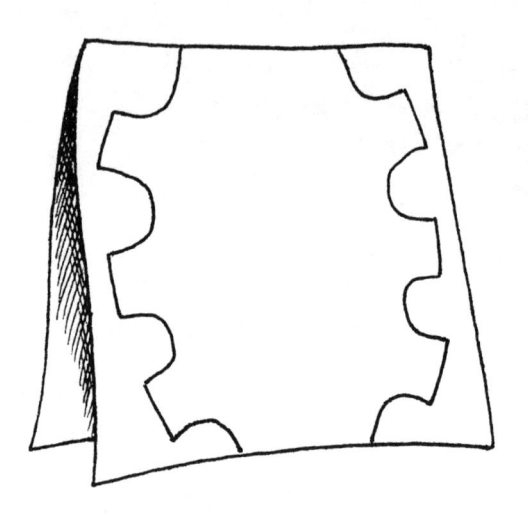

1. To make your flea, first fold a sheet of white felt in half, draw your flea pattern and cut it out. Then, glue the halves together, but leave the bottom open.

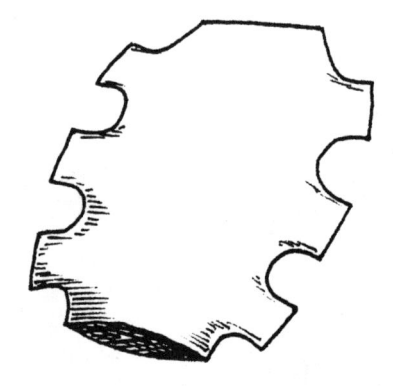

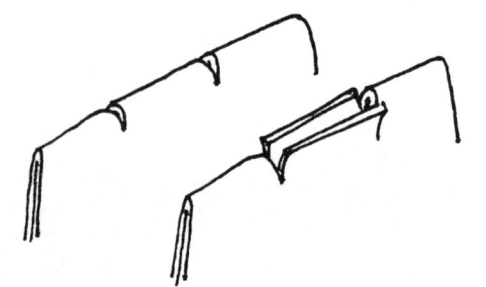

2. Next, cut a slit in the top by first cutting two small slits and then connecting them.

3. Now, make the feet by cutting half-circles out of black felt and gluing them to the legs.

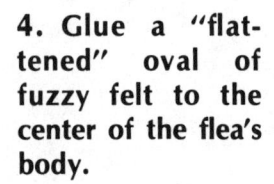

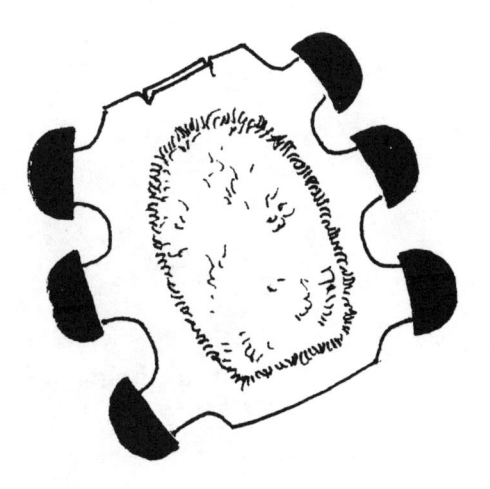

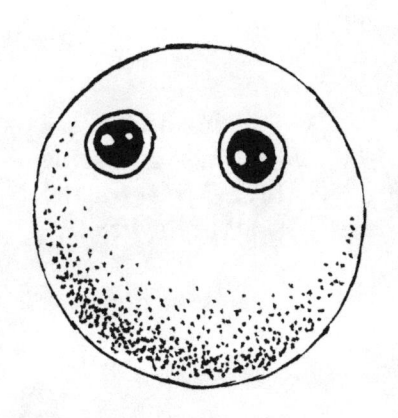

4. Glue a "flattened" oval of fuzzy felt to the center of the flea's body.

5. While the body dries, push two plastic eyes into a styrofoam ball head.

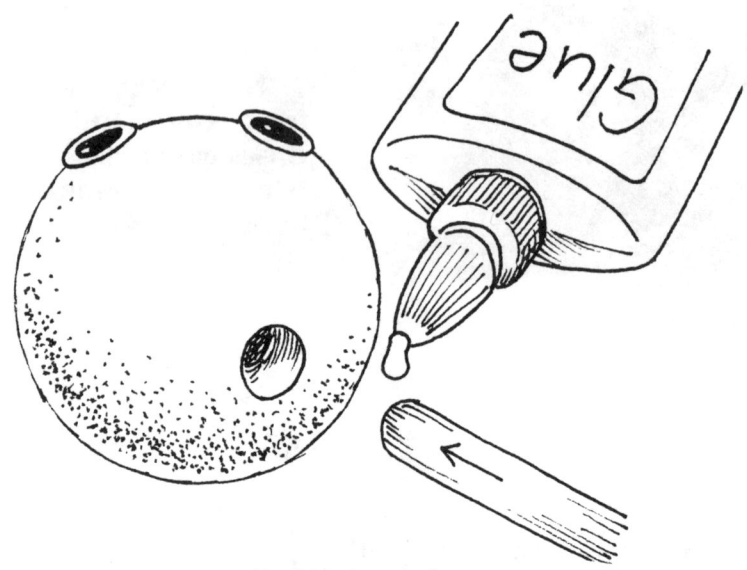

6. Next, make a hole in the bottom of the styrofoam ball about an inch deep and glue in a dowel.

7. Glue on a black felt smile and some fuzzy felt to the sides of the head.

Dusty's Flea Market 85

8. Take ⅓ of a pipe cleaner, bend it into a horseshoe shape, bend down the ends, and stick it into the head. Glue a pink felt nose to it.

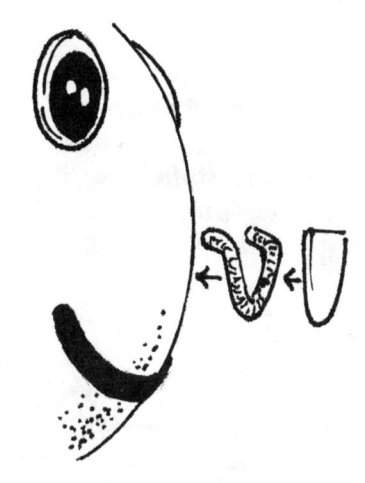

9. Use the rest of the pipe cleaner for feelers.

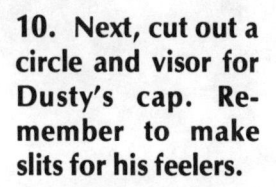

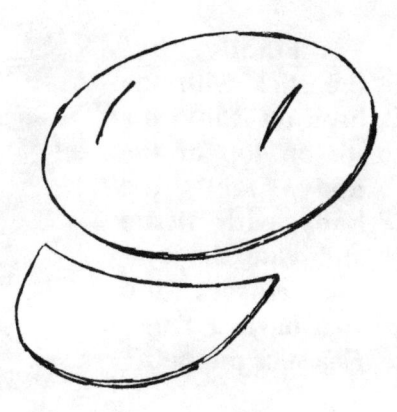

10. Next, cut out a circle and visor for Dusty's cap. Remember to make slits for his feelers.

11. Pin the visor to the head, then pin the cap on over some stuffing so it stands up.

12. Now, cut out and glue on a white "D" to Dusty's cap.

13. Finally, put the stick with the head on it into the slit on top of the body, stuff the body with tissue and glue the bottom closed, and you have a Dusty Flea stick puppet.

Mall E. Mouse

Where: Mice Mall. When: A Super Saturday Sales Day.
Puppeteers: Two. Time: 15 minutes.

Characters

Mall E. Mouse Jr. . . . A tiny mouse who thinks big
Mall E. Mouse . . . . Mally's father and owner
              of Mice Mall
Mom Mouse . . . . . . Mally's mother and manager
              of the Mice Cheese Shop
Le Cat. . . . . A fierce, fat cat who
              captures Mice Mall
Security Rat . . . . . . A tough rat who
              guards Mice Mall
Mice Shoppers. . . . . Mice who shop at Mice Mall

Music: "Alley Cat" can be played before play.

At Rise: The play takes place in Mice Mall, which is a large shopping complex. A tall mouse statue is pinned to the center of the backdrop curtain.

Above the mouse status is a sign which says, "MICE MALL," Mall E. Mouse, Owner. Under this sign is another sign which is flipped down later that says, "AND SON."

Large pots with colorful flowers are tacked across the edge of the stage.

(Curtain opens.)
(Music: "Alley Cat.")
(Mice Shoppers enter and cross the stage and exit as the music plays.)
(Security Rat enters and crosses the stage and exits.)

Mall E. Mouse: *(Enters.)* Ladies and gentlemice. May I have your attention? Thank you. I am Mall E. Mouse, the proud owner of Mice Mall. Today, in our fine shopping mall, we are having our Super Saturday Sales. *(Walks around the stage.)* Mouse-Mart has ten percent off on Mice designer jeans. Mouse and Hardware has twenty percent off on all its mouse hole diggers. Rats Drugs has long-tail Mouse curlers, two for the price of one. They also have Whisker Perfume, the big bottle size for ninety-eight cents. That's right, only ninety-eight cents.

At the Mouse Chocolate Shop they are giving away Pink Ears Bubble Gum. So, you early mice shoppers had better scurry before everything is nibbled up. Be sure to stop in at the Mice Cheese Shop. My wife is the manager of this shop and she makes mighty nice mice cheeses that melt in your mouth.

Mally: *(Enters.)* Hi, Dad. How's the big sale going?

Mall E. Mouse: It's going great, son.

Mally: Can I help you with the sales?

Mall E. Mouse: That is nice of you to offer, Mally. But, you are too small.

Mally: I know I'm small, but I could do something.

Mall E. Mouse: It takes a big, strong mouse to run Mice Mall.

Mally: I know, Dad, but there could be some—

Mall E. Mouse: I'm afraid you might get hurt.

Mall E. Mouse

MALLY: But, Dad, I could—

MALL E. MOUSE: I'm afraid you'd just be in the way.

MALLY: But, Dad, please—?

MALL E. MOUSE: Go have one of your mother's nice mice cheeses. *(Exits.)*

MALLY: I know I'm small, and Dad thinks I'm so small, I can do nothing at all.

MOM MOUSE: *(Enters, carrying a tray of mice cheeses.)* Mally, dear, what are you up to?

MALLY: Mom, can I help you in the Mice Cheese Shop?

MOM: That is sweet of you, Mally, but you are too small.

MALLY: I hate being small.

MOM: Someday you won't be so small.

MALLY: I'll always be small.

MOM: Don't fret, dear. Go play with that thing-a-ma-jig of yours. I have to take these mice cheeses to your father. Have you seen him?

MALLY: *(Points to where* MALL E. MOUSE *exited.)* He went that way.

MOM: Would you like a cheese, Mally, dear?

MALLY: Not now, Mom, but could I help carry the tray?

MOM: Oh, Mally. It's too heavy. You are too—

MALLY: I'm too small.

MOM: Be a good little mouse. *(Exits.)*

MALLY: *(Walks sadly around the stage.)* I'm small. I'm short. I'm small. I'm short. Wish I were big and tall.

SECURITY RAT: *(Enters.)* Hi there, Mally Mouse. Catch any cats lately. *(Laughs.)*

MALLY: Oh, hello, Security Rat. You are the one to catch the cats. Have you seen any lately?

SECURITY RAT: Naw! No cat in its right mind would attack Mice Mall. Not with me on duty.

MALLY: You'd bite off its tail, right?

SECURITY RAT: Right you are, sonny.

Puppets Le Cat (left) and Mall E. Mouse with "Cat-Mouse Game" (a prop) and two young puppeteers.

Mall E. Mouse

MALLY: May I help you patrol Mice Mall? Please, may I? Please?

SECURITY RAT: *(Laughs.)* You help me patrol Mice Mall? That's funny.

MALLY: I have sharp eyes. I could spot a shoplifter for you. I'd be great on a cat attack.

SECURITY RAT: You on a cat attack? A small mouse like you? You make me laugh. Ho! Ho! *(Laughs louder.)*

MALLY: It's not funny being small.

SECURITY RAT: You on a cat attack. That's rich. Thanks for the laugh. *(Exits.)*

MALLY: *(Walks sadly around the stage.)* I don't think I'll ever be big enough to do anything.

(Scratching sound is heard.)

MALLY: What was that?

(LE CAT pokes his head up and disappears.)

MALLY: I know somebody is watching me.

(LE CAT appears and disappears.)

MALLY: That somebody is making me shiver. That somebody is up to no good. I can feel it. *(Shivers.)* I've got the mouse shivers. My mouse shivers say — It's a cat!!!

LE CAT: *(Appears and disappears.)* Meow.

MALLY: It sounds like a cat.

LE CAT: *(Appears and disappears.)* Meow.

MALLY: It can't be a cat. Security Rat says no cat in its right mind would attack Mice Mall with him on duty.

(LE CAT appears and disappears.)

MALLY: Security Rat would bite off its tail, if a cat ever crept around here.

LE CAT: *(Appears and meows very loud.)* Meow! Meow!

MALLY: *(Is frozen to the spot.)* It *is* a cat! And, what a cat! W-W-Who are you?

LE CAT: *(Speaks with a French accent.)* I'm Le Cat. I'm a fat cat.

MALLY: *(Backs away from* LE CAT.*)* W-W-What are you doing here, Le Cat?

LE CAT: I am going to capture Mice Mall. But, before I do, I'm going to gobble you up. *(Runs to* MALLY.*)* I love *little* juicy mice.

MALLY: You aren't going to gobble *me* up. *(Runs offstage.)*

LE CAT: Where did that small fry go?

MALLY: *(Pops up.)* Here I am. You'd better watch out for Security Rat. He'll bite off your tail.

LE CAT: *(Leaps for* MALLY, *and* MALLY *disappears.)* I'm not afraid of Security Rat. He won't dare put a tooth on me.

MALLY: *(Pops up.)* Oh, go chase your tail.

MOM MOUSE: *(Enters.)* EEEEEK! A cat!

LE CAT: Ah! A mouse! *(Chases* MOM MOUSE.*)*

MOM MOUSE: EEEEEEEEEK! *(Disappears.)*

MALL E. MOUSE: *(Enters.)* Upon my word! A cat!

LE CAT: I have taken over Mice Mall.

MALL E. MOUSE: What a cat-astrophe!

LE CAT: I like small, juicy mice better, but I'm hungry. *(Chases* MALL E. MOUSE.*)* You will do.

MALL E. MOUSE: Mice Mall is doomed! *(Exits.)*

LE CAT: *(Looks where* MALL E. MOUSE *has disappeared.)* Where did that big mouse go?

SECURITY RAT: *(Enters.)* Mozzarella! A cat! A big, fierce cat!

MALLY: *(Pokes his head up.)* Watch out for Le Cat!

SECURITY RAT: Sh! Sh! *(Sneaks up on* LE CAT, *picks up his tail and bites it.)*

LE CAT: *(Yells.)* Yeeeow! YIKES!

MALLY: *(Pops up.)* I told you Security Rat would bite your tail.

LE CAT: Nobody is going to bite my tail and get away with it. Watch out, Rat! *(Chases* SECURITY RAT *off the stage.)*

Mall E. Mouse

MALLY: *(Enters.)* We have got to get rid of that cat. But how? *(Walks around the stage.)* Maybe I can think of a way. But, I'm too small. I can't do anything at all. But I do have brains. O.K., I'll use them. I know what I'll do. *(Calls to LE CAT.)* Here kitty, kitty. Come kitty. Nice kitty, handsome cat. Where are you?

LE CAT: *(Enters.)* Are you calling me, you little shrimp?

MALLY: Yes, Mr. Le Cat.

LE CAT: What's on your mind, besides squeaking away from me?

MALLY: You look like a smart cat.

LE CAT: I am a smart cat.

MALLY: I wonder if you are smart enough to play my Cat-Mouse Video game.

LE CAT: I'm smart enough to play any video game. I'm not called King Video Cat for nothing.

MALLY: O.K. I'll be right back. *(Exits.)*

LE CAT: What a dumb mouse. What a small, dumb mouse, but that dumb, small mouse will make a tasty treat.

MALLY: *(Enters, pushing the Cat-Mouse game.)* Help me, Le Cat.

LE CAT: *(Pulls the Cat-Mouse game.)* Such a weak mouse. You're no Mighty Mouse. How do you play this Cat-Mouse game?

MALLY: *(Points to cat.)* See the big cat on the board?

LE CAT: He looks like me.

MALLY: The cat tries to gobble up the mice before they go down into their mouse holes.

LE CAT: Sounds simple enough.

MALLY: The hard part is you have to catch all the mice before the bell rings. When the bell rings, and you haven't caught the mice, you have to play another game. It costs a quarter a game.

LE CAT: Put it on my bill. I can't wait to start playing.

MALLY: Go ahead and play, and I'll keep track of what you owe. I can do it in my head without a computer.

(The cat and mice move on the board as LE CAT *plays the game. Bell rings.)*

MALLY: You have got to start over.

LE CAT: *(Plays the game.)* I know. Put another quarter on the tab.

*(*LE CAT *plays the game. Bell rings.)*

MALLY: The bell rang.

LE CAT: I heard it! *(Continues playing the game.)*

MALLY: You haven't caught one mouse yet.

LE CAT: I know! I know! *(Plays Cat-Mouse.)*

(Music: "Alley Cat" plays in background as LE CAT *continues playing the game. The bell rings.* LE CAT *continues to play, and the bell rings again.)*

MALLY: You're going to be broke, and you look awfully tired.

LE CAT: *(Continues to play.)* Who cares? I am going to win. No video game has been invented that can outsmart King Video Cat.

(Bell rings.)

MALLY: Your eyes are glued to the game, Le Cat.

LE CAT: I don't care. I've got to play until I win.

MALLY: That will be forever, because you will never win my video game.

LE CAT: Be quiet, shrimp.

*(*LE CAT *plays the game. Bell continues to ring. Music fades.)*

SECURITY RAT: *(Enters.)* What have you done to Le Cat? His eyes are glued to that thing of yours.

MALLY: I captured him with my Cat-Mouse video game.

SECURITY RAT: Well, I'll be a Parmesan cheese, if you ain't the smartest little mouse I've ever seen. You are so smart, you can patrol Mice Mall with me anytime.

MALLY: Really, Security Rat?

SECURITY RAT: Really. You are the best cat catcher I've ever seen with that game of yours. *(Exits.)*

MOM MOUSE: *(Enters.)* Mally, get away from that cat!

MALLY: Don't worry, Mom. I have Le Cat stuck to my Cat-Mouse video game. He will never leave.

MOM MOUSE: How can you do that?

MALLY: Mom, I've got Le Cat hooked to the game. He will never bother Mice Mall again.

MOM MOUSE: Mally, you are smart. I'm so proud of you.

MALLY: Thanks, Mom.

MOM MOUSE: A smart mouse like you can help me with my mice cheeses any time.

MALLY: Thanks, Mom. I'd like to help you.

MOM: I'll go and make some mice cheeses right now. With Le Cat captured, Mice Mall will be busy again. *(Exits.)*

MALL E. MOUSE: *(Enters.)* Mally! Are you all right?

MALLY: Sure I am, Dad. I have captured Le Cat.

MALL E. MOUSE: How can he be captured? He's standing there by that thing-a-ma-bob you've been working on for so long.

MALLY: He won't ever stop playing. My Cat-Mouse video game has got him glued.

MALL E. MOUSE: You have saved Mice Mall. I am proud of you.

MALLY: Thanks, Dad.

MALL E. MOUSE: Wait here. *(Exits.)*

MALLY: Wonder what Dad's up to?

(MALL E. MOUSE enters, carrying a stick.)

MALLY: What's the stick for?

MALL E. MOUSE: Watch! *(Flips down a sign under MALL E. MOUSE sign. It says, AND SON.*

MALLY: Wow, Dad! That's great!

MALL E. MOUSE: You may be small, son, but you are big enough to be a partner of Mice Mall. From now on MALL E. MOUSE and SON will run Mice Mall.

MALLY: Way to go, Dad.

MALL E. MOUSE: *(Shakes hands with* MALLY.*)* Way to go, son. *(They exit.)*

(Optional: MICE SHOPPERS *enter and cross the stage and exit as the music plays.)*

*(*SECURITY RAT *enters and crosses the stage and exits.)*

MALLY: *(Enters and talks to the audience.)* Ladies and gentlemice. May I have your attention? I am the son of Mall E. Mouse. *(Points to sign "AND SON.")* Today is our Super Saturday Sales at Mice Mall. After a brief Cat Attack, we are continuing our sales. You mice shoppers better scurry before all the great buys are nibbled up.

We also have a very special attraction in Mice Mall, a first. We are presenting the furious, mouse-eating, Le Cat, playing my new video game, called Cat-Mouse. It costs a quarter to see him play the game. Don't be afraid. Step right up. Le Cat is glued to the spot. He can't get away. Come one, come all, to Mice Mall.

(Curtain closes.)

Props: Signs: MICE MALL; MALL E. MOUSE, OWNER; AND SON; tray with mice cheeses; stick; four large flower pots with colorful flowers; mouse statue; bell; the Cat-Mouse video game; scratching sound.

Production Notes: The children can make mice masks and cat masks. The masks can be made from paper bags, cutting out eyes and mouths, and painting on eyelashes, whiskers, mouths and eyes. Ears can be cut out of cardboard and glued to the paper bags—big, round ears for the mice, and pointed ears for the cat. Glue a small, black yarn nose on the bag for the cat's nose. For the mice, add a yarn ball on the end of a cardboard cone.

Mall E. Mouse

Cardboard masks attached to a stick or a tongue depresser can be painted with mice and cat faces. Cut out the eyes so the children can see. The children can hold these masks up to their faces.

The children can make mice shopper puppets, and play the Cat-Mouse video game.

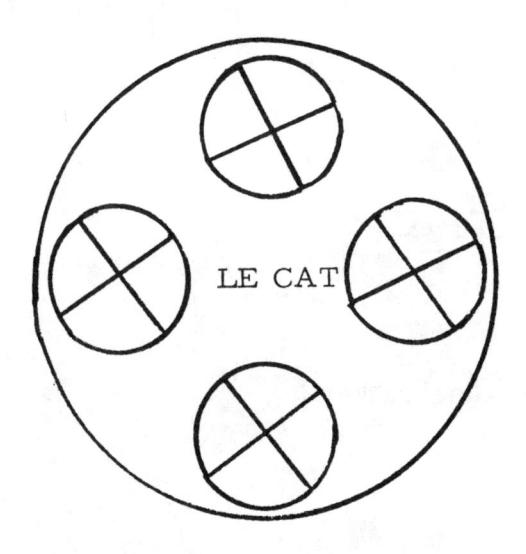

The Cat-Mouse Video Game

The children form a large circle. With chalk, draw four round "mouse hole" circles, about two feet in diameter, across from each other inside the circle. A child stands on each circle. They are the mice. Le Cat stands in the center of the circle.

When the bell rings, the mice scamper to the next mice hole circle, running clockwise. Le Cat tries to catch a mouse before it reaches a mouse hole circle. This is repeated until a mouse is caught. Then, that mouse becomes Le Cat and the first Le Cat goes into the large circle of children. The game is played again.

A Mouse Stick Puppet

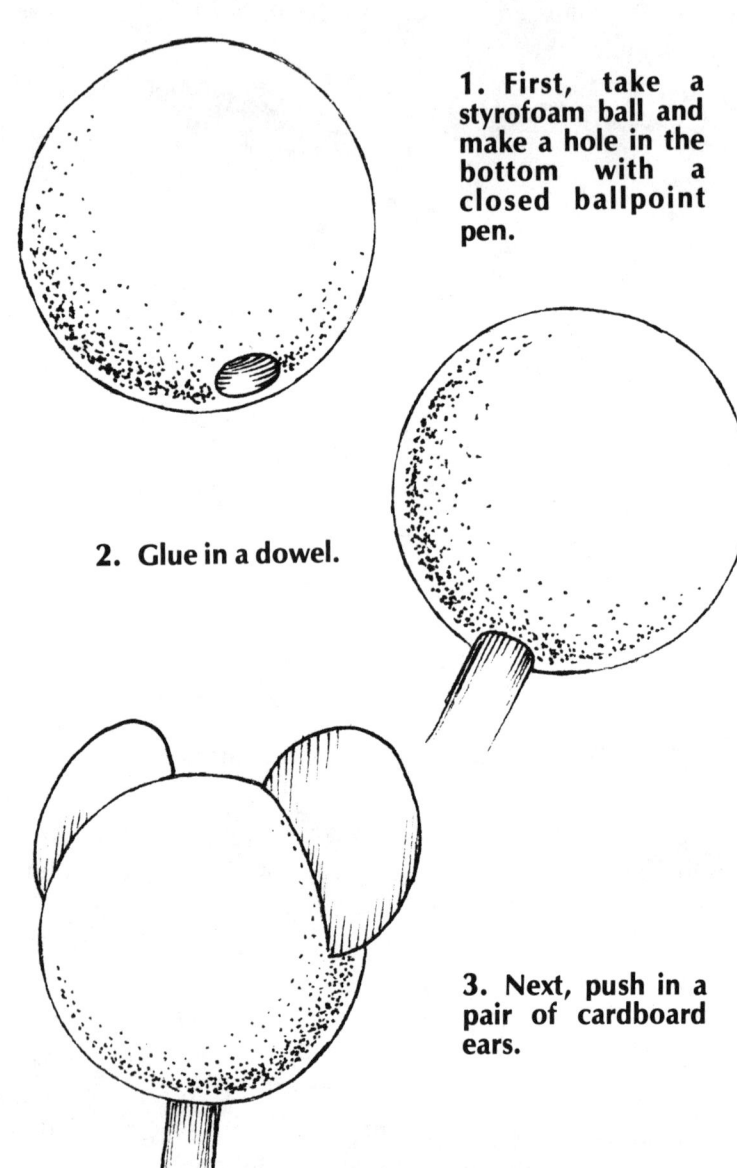

1. First, take a styrofoam ball and make a hole in the bottom with a closed ballpoint pen.

2. Glue in a dowel.

3. Next, push in a pair of cardboard ears.

Mall E. Mouse

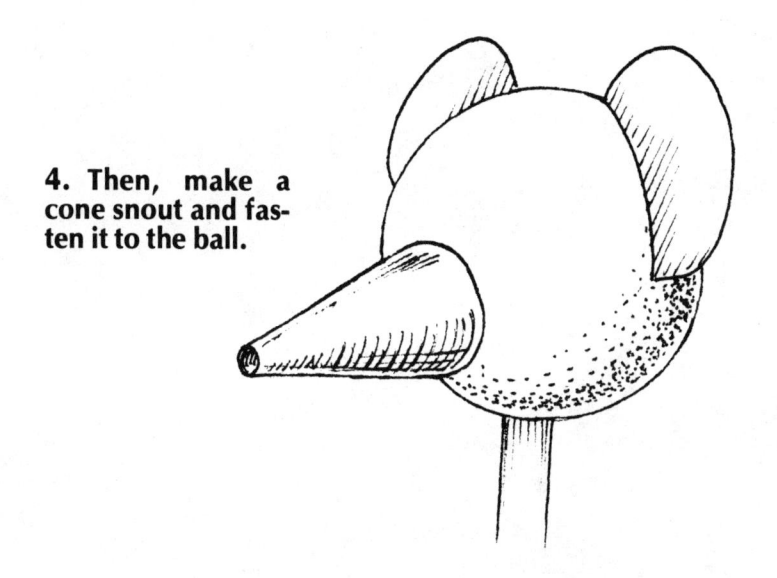

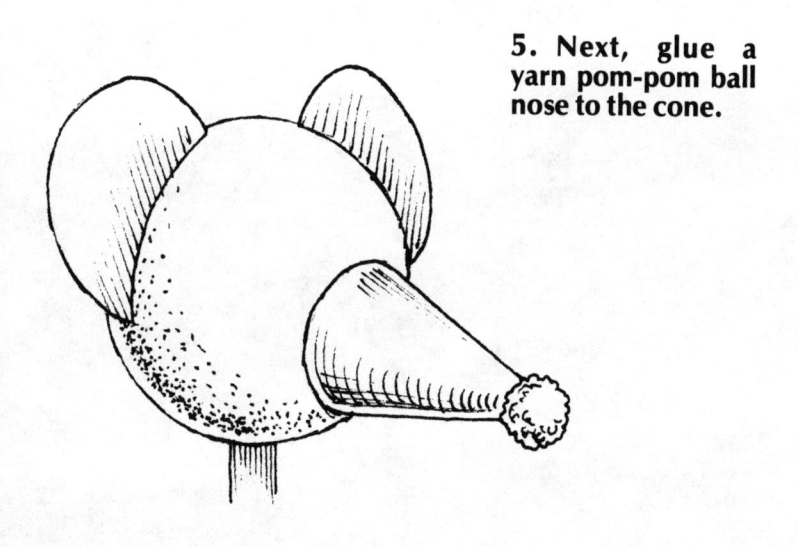

4. Then, make a cone snout and fasten it to the ball.

5. Next, glue a yarn pom-pom ball nose to the cone.

6. Push in a set of plastic eyes.

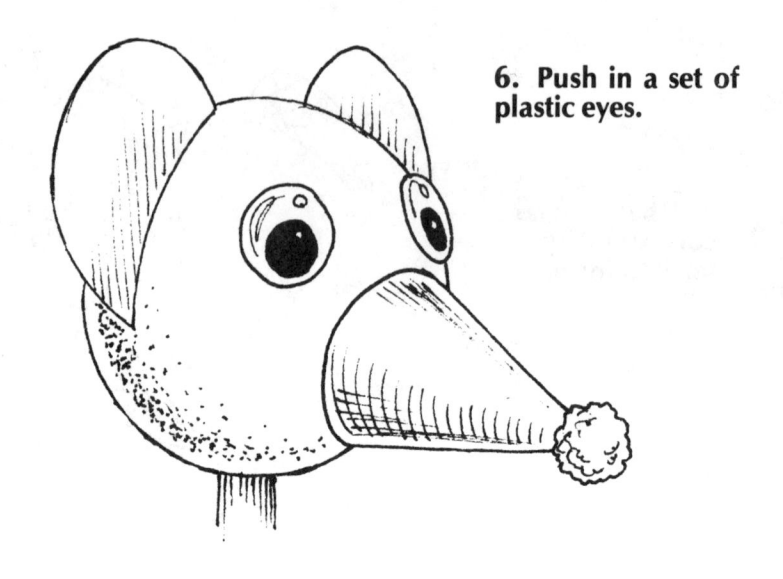

7. For a final touch, add a bow tie to your puppet and...

...you have a Mouse!

Ghosts in the Pumpkin Patch

WHERE: A pumpkin patch. WHEN: Halloween. PUPPETEERS: Three. TIME: 20 minutes.

CHARACTERS

PROFESSOR PELVEDERE POMPOUS ... A conceited professor
PRISCILLA POMPOUS .. A wife who finds out she's important too
LIVER HEAD .... A slippery crook
PRUNE FACE .... A wrinkly crook
OFFICER DUTY ...... A policeman who does his duty
RACCOON .... A furry animal

At Rise: On stage there is a fence with pumpkins growing in front of it. Liver Head and Prune Face race in out of breath. They keep looking back. Prune Face is carrying a money bag. The two robbers wear black eye masks.

Liver Head: Officer Duty almost got us.

Prune Face: You can say that again.

Liver Head: Officer Duty almost got us.

Prune Face: Knock it off, Liver Head.

Liver Head: Well, he almost did get us, Prune Face.

Prune Face: I know. Look! There's Officer Duty heading this way. Take off, Liver Head! *(Runs offstage.)*

Liver Head: I'm ahead of you, Prune Face. *(Runs offstage.)*

Officer Duty: *(Enters.)* O.K., you turkeys. I'm on your tail. *(Exits.)*

Prune Face: *(Runs across stage.)* Run for your life, Liver Head.

Liver Head: *(Runs across stage.)* I'm running for my life, Prune Face.

Officer Duty: *(Chases robbers.)* Those two miserable robbers! They will not get away from me. *(Exits.)*

Prune Face: *(Enters.)* We side-tracked Officer Duty.

Liver Head: *(Enters.)* That we did, Prune Face. That we did.

Prune Face: But it won't be for long. *(Holds up money bag.)* We've got to hide this money bag.

Liver Head: Right, Prune Face. We've got to hide that money bag.

Prune Face: I just said that, Liver Head.

Liver Head: Right. You just said that.

Prune Face: Knock it off, Liver Head. Cut out the gab. Get thinking. Where shall we hide it?

Liver Head: How should I know?

Prune Head: You should know, you doublehead. Think of a good hiding place, now!

Liver Head: It's too much trouble. Why don't we take the money back to the bank where we stole it?

Prune Face: That's the dumbest idea you've ever had, and you have had some dumb ones.

LIVER HEAD: Oh! Oh! Hide the money bag, anywhere! Here comes Officer Duty.

PRUNE FACE: I'll hide it under the pumpkins. *(Puts money bag back of pumpkins and exits.)*

LIVER HEAD: Good idea. *(Exits.)*

OFFICER DUTY: *(Runs in, out of breath.)* I'm gaining on those two crooks. They must have come this way. Anyone seen two slippery characters? *(Asks audience if they have seen the two crooks.)* I'll get 'em! *(Exits.)*

PROFESSOR: *(Enters, carrying a shovel.)* Priscilla!

PRISCILLA: *(Enters with shovel.)* I'm coming, Pelvedere!

PROFESSOR: You are slower than a cow's tail.

PRISCILLA: *(Shakes her head.)* I am not!

PROFESSOR: A big dig is no place for a woman like you.

PRISCILLA: What's the matter with me?

PROFESSOR: Look at you. No archaeologist in his right mind would wear what you are wearing to a big dig—that funny hat, that funny dress.

PRISCILLA: *(Walks and looks at the pumpkins.)* This pumpkin patch is a pretty place. I'm going to take a pumpkin home and make a jack-o-lantern for Halloween.

PROFESSOR: Blast the pumpkins, Priscilla! Get digging if you are going to.

PRISCILLA: Where shall I dig?

PROFESSOR: How should I know? ... Anywhere!

PRISCILLA: What are we digging for?

PROFESSOR: By my expert calculations, I believe there is an Indian burial ground in this very pumpkin patch.

PRISCILLA: Oh, Pelvedere! How exciting. We may discover an Indian treasure. Let's see. I think I will dig over there. *(Lifts her shovel and knocks PROFESSOR down.)*

(PROFESSOR gets up slowly.)

PRISCILLA: No, I guess I will dig over there. Pelvedere, I don't know where to dig. *(Lifts her shovel and knocks down the PROFESSOR again.)*

Professor Pelvedere Pompous, noted puppet, and young puppet master.

Ghosts in the Pumpkin Patch

PROFESSOR: *(Gets up and shouts at* PRISCILLA.*)* Priscilla! You nin-com-poop!

PRISCILLA: Whatever is the matter, Pelvedere?

PROFESSOR: You knocked me down with your shovel. Not once, but twice! You are the biggest nin-com-poop I have ever known.

PRISCILLA: I'm sorry, Pelvedere. Did I hurt you?

PROFESSOR: Forget it! I'm going to dig. I might dig up an Indian burial ground of the Chippewa, Ottawa, or Pottawatomi Indians. *(Starts digging.)*

PRISCILLA: Who?

PROFESSOR: The Chippewa, Ottawa, or Pottawatomi Indians.

PRISCILLA: Oh, the Chippewa, Ottawa, or Pottawatomi?

PROFESSOR: Yes, the Chippewa, Ottawa, or Pottawatomi.

PRISCILLA: *(Sings the words and does a little Indian dance.)* Oh, the Chippewa, Ottawa, or Pottawatomi.

PROFESSOR: *(Sings out the words very loud and gives a war whoop along with some Indian dancing.)* Oh, the Chippewa, Ottawa, or Pottawatomi.

PRISCILLA: *(Gives a war whoop and dances up a storm.)* Hey, the Chippewa, Ottawa, or Pottawatomi.

PROFESSOR: *(Stops dancing.)* Priscilla!!!

PRISCILLA: *(Stops dancing.)* Yes, Pelvedere?

PROFESSOR: Stop that Indian dancing. You are driving me crazy.

PRISCILLA: Sorry, dear. *(Starts to dig.)*

PROFESSOR: *(Digs without saying anything, then —)* Priscilla! I've hit something!

PRISCILLA: *(Runs to* PROFESSOR.*)* What, Pelvedere? What?

PROFESSOR: Something important. I may have made an archaeological discovery and I will be famous.

PRISCILLA: Oh, Pelvedere! How wonderful!

PROFESSOR: *(Picks up a pottery jar.)* Look, Priscilla!

PRISCILLA: *(Looks at jar.)* What is it?

PROFESSOR: *(Holds up jar.)* I think it is an ancient Indian water jar.

PRISCILLA: You do?

PROFESSOR: Yes, I do. Put your shovel down and hold it very carefully while I dig some more. There may be something else down here.

PRISCILLA: Yes, dear. *(Lays down her shovel and takes jar.)*

PROFESSOR: I don't want anything to happen to my fantastic find.

PRISCILLA: No, dear.

(RACCOON enters; PROFESSOR continues digging.)

PRISCILLA: Find anything more, Pelvedere?

(RACCOON creeps nearer to PRISCILLA.)

PROFESSOR: No! *(Continues digging.)*

PRISCILLA: *(Sees raccoon and screams, and drops the pottery jar.)* A bear! A bear!

PROFESSOR: Priscilla! My Indian water jar! You dropped my Indian water jar!

PRISCILLA: *(Points to RACCOON.)* A bear, Pelvedere! A big, furry bear.

PROFESSOR: You nin-com-poop! That is not a big, furry bear. That is a small, furry raccoon.

PRISCILLA: It is?

PROFESSOR: It is, and raccoons will not hurt you.

PRISCILLA: They won't?

PROFESSOR: They won't. You are hopeless. *(Looks at pottery jar.)* It's a good thing for you the Indian water jar didn't break.

PRISCILLA: I'm glad, too, Pelvedere. I want you to be famous.

PROFESSOR: Get digging, Priscilla!

PRISCILLA: Yes, dear. *(Digs and sings.)* You've got to dig big, You've got to dig big. You've got to dig big. Dig! Dig! Dig! Dig! Dig!

Ghosts in the Pumpkin Patch

Professor: *(Yells at Priscilla.)* Priscilla!
Priscilla: *(Stops singing.)* Yes, dear?
Professor: Never mind. Get digging.
Priscilla: Yes, dear.
(Professor and Priscilla continue digging.)
Prune Face: *(Enters quietly.)* Sh!
Liver Head: *(Enters quietly.)* Sh!
Professor: *(Stops digging.)* Did you hear something?
Priscilla: *(Stops digging.)* Only the bear, I mean, the raccoon in the pumpkins.
Professor: O.K. Quit the gab and go back to digging.
Priscilla: Yes, dear.
(Professor and Priscilla continue digging.)
Prune Face: *(Whispers.)* We've got to get our money bag back.
Liver Head: How?
Prune Face: Sh! They might hear you.
Liver Head: What are those two kooks digging for, anyhow?
Prune Face: I heard them talking about some Indian treasures. I think the professor found an old pot.
Liver Head: They will have a real treasure if they find our money bag. *(Laughs.)*
Prune Face: Sh! We've got to get rid of them so we can get it back.
Liver Head: Right! We've got to get rid of them so we can get our money bag back.
Prune Face: Follow me, Liver Head. I have a plan. *(Exits.)*
Liver Head: I'm following you, Prune Face. *(Exits.)*
Priscilla: What did you say, Pelvedere?
Professor: I didn't say anything.
Priscilla: Then who did?
Professor: You are hearing things, Priscilla. Next thing you'll be telling me that you are seeing Indian ghosts.

PRISCILLA: *(Drops her shovel and yells.)* Ghosts!

PROFESSOR: Never fear, Priscilla, dear. There're no such things as Indian ghosts.

PRISCILLA: But, Pelvedere. I read a book about Indians once and it said Indian ghosts will come back to haunt you, if you disturb their burial ground. You just dug up an old Indian water jar.

PROFESSOR: Nonsense, Priscilla! That's a lot of rot! Get digging. *(Continues digging.)*

PRISCILLA: I hope you are right. *(Continues digging.)*

PRUNE FACE: *(Appears, dressed in a white sheet with an Indian band and feather around his head. There is a black mask over his eyes, glued to the sheet.)* O-O-O-O-O-O-O!

(RACCOON runs off very fast.)

PRISCILLA: *(Shakes.)* W-W-What was that?

PROFESSOR: P-P-Probably a hoot owl. Keep digging.

LIVER HEAD: *(Appears in same costume.)* O-O-O-O-O-O!

PRISCILLA: There! I heard it again. Pelvedere, I'm afraid! *(Cries.)*

PROFESSOR: *(Stutters.)* S-S-Stop talking and g-g-get digging.

LIVER HEAD AND PRUNE FACE: *(Fly around the stage.)* O-O-O-O-O-O!

PRISCILLA: *(Points at the ghosts.)* Look, Pelvedere! Ghosts!

PROFESSOR: What rot are you talking, Priscilla?

PRISCILLA: *(Points to Indian ghosts again.)* Ghosts, Pelvedere! Real ghosts! Real, live ghosts! Look!

PROFESSOR: You know there's no such thing as real, live ghosts.

PRISCILLA: But look, Pelvedere!

PROFESSOR: Ghosts! *(Faints.)*

PRISCILLA: *(Runs to PROFESSOR and shakes him.)* Don't pass out, Pelvedere. Don't leave me alone with these ghosts, Pelvedere, please!

Ghosts in the Pumpkin Patch

LIVER HEAD AND PRUNE FACE: *(Fly around.)* O-O-O-O-O!

PRISCILLA: What am I to do?

LIVER HEAD AND PRUNE FACE: O-O-O-O-O-O!

PRISCILLA: *(Waves her arms at the Indian ghosts.)* I know there's really no such thing as Indian ghosts. I'm not going to let them frighten me.

LIVER HEAD: *(Waves his arms at* PRISCILLA.*)* O-O-O-O-O-O!

PRISCILLA: You are not going to frighten me, you Indian spook. *(Picks up her shovel and swings it at* LIVER HEAD, *knocking him out.)*

PRUNE FACE: O-O-O-O-O-O!

PRISCILLA: You don't frighten me, either. *(Knocks out* PRUNE FACE *with her shovel.)*

PROFESSOR: *(Gets up slowly and rubs his eyes.)* W-W-What happened?

PRISCILLA: You fainted.

PROFESSOR: I did?

PRISCILLA: I knocked out the two Indian ghosts.

PROFESSOR: You did? How?

PRISCILLA: *(Raises her shovel.)* With my shovel. Let's see who's under the sheets. *(Lays shovel down and pulls sheets from the crooks.)*

PROFESSOR: No! No! Priscilla, wait! Leave those ghosts alone!

OFFICER DUTY: *(Enters.)* There you are, you slippery Liver Head and you wrinkly Prune Face.

PRISCILLA: Oh, hello, Officer Duty.

OFFICER DUTY: Who knocked out these two miserable crooks?

PRISCILLA: I did.

OFFICER DUTY: *(Pulls up first* PRUNE FACE, *and then* LIVER HEAD.*)* You are to be congratulated, Mrs. Pompous. These two crooks are Public Enemies No. 1 and 2.

LIVER HEAD: Did you see my picture in the post office? Wasn't it great?

PRUNE FACE: You talk too much, Liver Head.

LIVER HEAD: I talk too much, Prune Face?

PRUNE FACE: That's what I said, Liver Head.

OFFICER DUTY: Both of you turkeys keep quiet. I'll read you your rights later.

PRISCILLA: What did they do, Officer Duty?

OFFICER DUTY: They held up the Money Tree National Bank, and you will get a reward for capturing them.

PRISCILLA: I will?

PROFESSOR: She will?

OFFICER DUTY: Yes, and whoever finds the money will receive another reward. Where's the money bag, boys?

PRUNE FACE: Search me.

LIVER HEAD: Search me.

OFFICER DUTY: I will. *(Searches first* LIVER HEAD, *then* PRUNE FACE.*)* They are clean.

LIVER HEAD: Mother taught me to take a bath.

PRUNE FACE: Knock it off, Liver Head.

LIVER HEAD: Knock it off yourself, Prune Face.

OFFICER DUTY: The money is probably long gone. Come on, off to jail you go. You were very brave, Mrs. Pompous. *(Exits with* LIVER HEAD *and* PRUNE FACE.*)*

PRISCILLA: Thank you, Officer Duty.

PROFESSOR: *(*I'd like to find that money bag with all the money. *(Picks up shovel and digs.)*

PRISCILLA: So would I. *(Picks up shovel and digs.)*

*(*RACCOON *enters and walks across the stage and exits.)*

PRISCILLA: Oh, Pelvedere! I hit something.

PROFESSOR: *(Goes to* PRISCILLA.*)* What? What?

PRISCILLA: I don't know. *(Puts down shovel.)*

PROFESSOR: Let me see. *(Holds up an old sneaker and yells.)* You nin-com-poop! It's an old sneaker!

PRISCILLA: Oh dear, I'm so disappointed, but I won't give up. Those crooks may have hidden the money bag in this very pumpkin patch. *(Continues digging.)*

Ghosts in the Pumpkin Patch

PROFESSOR: Nonsense, Priscilla! I am dead tired. I'm going to rest. *(Falls asleep and snores.)*

PRISCILLA: I'm going to dig, dig, dig, dig, dig.

(RACCOON enters and walks across stage and exits.)

PRISCILLA: *(Shouts.)* Oh, Pelvedere!

PROFESSOR: *(Sits up.)* What?

PRISCILLA: I found something!

PROFESSOR: Another old sneaker? Let me sleep! *(Lays down again.)*

PRISCILLA: No, it isn't. *(Puts down shovel and holds up money bag.)* It's the money bag.

PROFESSOR: *(Jumps up excitedly.)* The money bag!

PRISCILLA: Yes, the Money Tree National Bank money bag, and I found it. I will get the reward.

PROFESSOR: Think you are pretty smart, don't you?

PRISCILLA: Yes, I do.

PROFESSOR: Well, I found an Indian water jar.

PRISCILLA: Yes, you did. But, I found the money, money, money bag.

PROFESSOR: Priscilla, we are going home.

PRISCILLA: *(Holds up money bag.)* Good. Then I can go shopping, as soon as I get the reward. I can buy dresses, hats, furs and jewelry—all I like. I may even buy you a tie.

PRISCILLA: Oh, rot, Priscilla! Who cares? *(Holds up pottery jar.)* I will be famous with my discovery.

PRISCILLA: *(Looks at jar.)* Pelvedere!

PROFESSOR: What now?

PRISCILLA: Look at the bottom of your Indian water jar.

PROFESSOR: Why?

PRISCILLA: Because, Pelvedere, dear, it says, "Made in Japan." That's no Indian water jar.

PROFESSOR: Stop your chatter, Priscilla. We are going home! Immediately!

PRISCILLA: Yes, Pelvedere, as soon as I pick a pumpkin. I will have the prettiest jack-o-lantern in our neighborhood.

(Picks up a pumpkin.) I'm ready to go home now, Pelvedere. *(Exits.)*

PROFESSOR: Yes, Priscilla. *(Exits.)*
(RACCOON runs across stage.)
(Curtain closes.)

Props: Pumpkins; Indian water jar; two shovels; money bag; sneaker; two black eye masks; tom-tom (for backstage).

Production Notes: PRISCILLA wears a fancy dress and a feather boa around her neck. She wears necklaces and a large flowered hat. PROFESSOR wears a khaki outfit and a pith helmet. He has a small, black mustache.

A Ghost Dance may follow for the children who have made ghost puppets. *Music:* "War Whoops and Medicine Songs" (Chippewa), by Ethnic Folkways. You can add your own tom-toms and bells. Also, blue lighting will give a ghostly effect to the ghost scene.

Needed for Ghost Puppets: Foam ball; dowel stick; stick-in plastic eyes; papier mâché (ready-made: Celluclay — just add water); glue; white sheeting.

**See intructions for making
Indian Ghost puppet on pages 113–115.**

An Indian Ghost

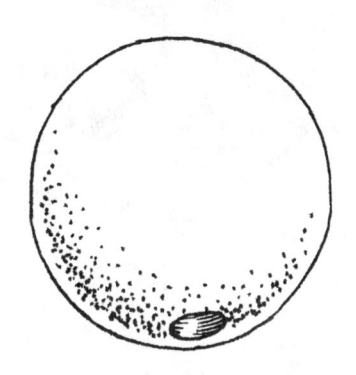

1. First, with a closed ballpoint pen, make a hole in the bottom of a styrofoam ball.

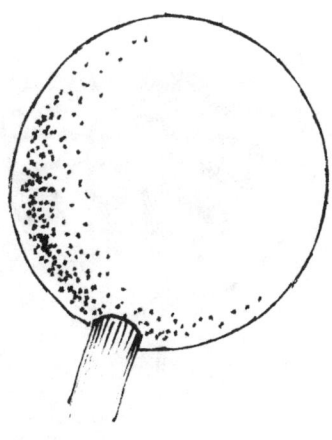

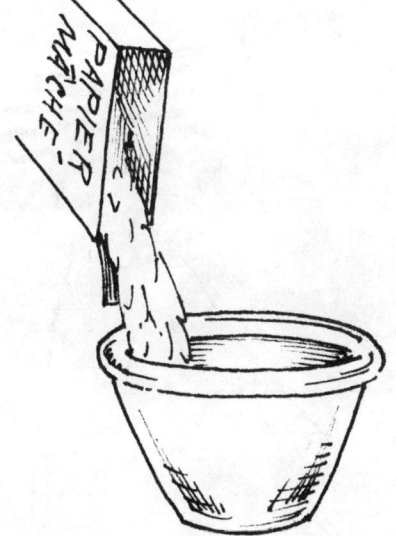

2. Glue a dowel into the hole.

3. Next, mix up some papier mâché (you can make your own, but ready-made is easiest). You can also use gray modeling clay.

4. With the papier mâché or clay, make an Indian face, as ghostly as you can. Let it dry overnight.

5. Paint this face with white acrylic paint. When it is dry, paint Indian designs on it.

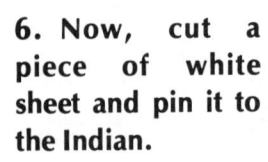

6. Now, cut a piece of white sheet and pin it to the Indian.

Ghosts in the Pumpkin Patch 115

(Indian designs and facial expression can be anything you like.)

7. Add an Indian headband and a feather and you have an Indian Ghost to fly around and scare people!

Booker's Library Party

WHERE: On a shelf in the library. WHEN: Any time.
PUPPETEERS: Two. TIME: 10 minutes.

CHARACTERS

BOOKER............ A handsome book full of facts and fiction
BOOKWORM......... A library bookworm
ROARY............. A noisy lion
STICKY ICKY........ A messy girl
MARKER............ A fellow who likes to mark books

At Rise: Booker and Bookworm are talking about Booker's Library Party. They are on a library shelf in the _____ Library. The background has the backs of books showing. There is a paper chain hanging across the books.

BOOKWORM: Gosh, Booker, that was a super idea of yours to have a library party.
BOOKER: Thanks, Bookworm. Parties are fun, and I think a library party will be lots of fun.

BOOKWORM: Me, too. That's a neat paper chain you made for decorating the library for the party.

BOOKER: Thanks, Bookworm. They're really easy to make, though.

ROARY: *(Roars offstage.)* Grrrrrrr!

BOOKWORM: WWWWWWhat was that?

BOOKER: Sounds like a lion roaring.

ROARY: *(Enters.)* Grrrrrr!

BOOKER: *(Points to Roary.)* See! It is a lion roaring!

ROARY: *(Roars very loud.)* Grrrrr!!!

BOOKER: Sh, Mr. Lion! You are not supposed to roar in the library.

BOOKWORM: That's right. You are supposed to talk softly in the library.

ROARY: Me not roar? Who ever heard of a lion not roaring? Grrrrr! *(Roars again.)*

BOOKER: *(Puts his hand to his mouth.)* Sh! Sh!

BOOKWORM: *(Puts her hand to her mouth.)* Sh! Sh!

ROARY: Roary, the lion, will never shhh! *(Roars again.)* Grrrrrr!

BOOKER: *(Waves his hands at* ROARY.*)* Go away, Roary!

ROARY: I will not go away! *(Roars again.)* Grrrrrr!

BOOKWORM: *(Waves her hands.)* Shoo! Shoo!

ROARY: I will not SHHHOOOO! Besides, I heard you were having a big party in the library. I love parties. I roar a lot at parties.

BOOKER: I am sorry, Roary, but you are not invited to my party.

BOOKWORM: You didn't receive an invitation, did you?

ROARY: No, but the king of the jungle doesn't need an invitation. I go wherever I please. *(Roars again.)* Grrrrr!

BOOKER: Well, you are not welcome at my library party. You are too noisy.

ROARY: Is that so? You make me mad. I could tear every page out of you, you know.

A Whistle-Stop puppet conductor, and friend.

Booker's Library Party

BOOKWORM: Oh, no, you don't. *(Pushes ROARY off the library shelf.)* Off the shelf you go.

BOOKER: That was quick thinking, Bookworm. I am glad he has gone.

BOOKWORM: I took him by surprise. I'm glad he's gone, too.

STICKY ICKY: *(Enters, licking a big lollipop.)* Hello, Hello. Hello.

BOOKER: Who are you?

STICKY ICKY: My name is Sticky Icky. I heard you were having a fun party here in the library. So, here I am. I love parties!

BOOKWORM: Your name fits you. You are a mess. Look at your face, your dress, and your hands!

STICKY ICKY: What's a little catsup, mustard, bubble gum or marshmallow between friends? *(Looks at her hands.)*

BOOKER: You look awfully sticky to me.

STICKY ICKY: So?

BOOKWORM: So, you are not wanted in this library.

BOOKER: You will mess everything up.

STICKY ICKY: My! Aren't we fussy? *(Goes for BOOKER.)* Wait until I get my hands on you.

BOOKER: Don't come near me with those sticky hands. You will stick my pages together.

BOOKWORM: *(Pushes STICKY ICKY off the library shelf.)* No Sticky Ickys around here.

BOOKER: You did it again. Thanks, Bookworm.

BOOKWORM: That's O.K.

BOOKER: You are a real friend.

BOOKWORM: That's what friends are for.

MARKER: *(Enters, carrying a big yellow marker.)* There's nothing like a good friend, I always say.

BOOKER: Who are you?

MARKER: I would like to introduce myself. My name is Percival Marker, the Third, but everyone calls me Marker.

Are you the Booker who is throwing the big bash today in the library?

BOOKER: Yes, I'm Booker, and this is my friend, Bookworm.

MARKER: Pleased to meet you both. Say, Booker, you do look interesting. *(Moves to BOOKER.)* Let me get a closer look at you.

BOOKER: Hey, what are you doing?

MARKER: *(Marks BOOKER with his yellow marker.)* I'm marking you.

BOOKER: Well, cut it out! I don't like being marked. Besides, if you mark me, nobody can read me.

MARKER: *(Keeps marking BOOKER.)* Picky! Picky!

BOOKER: I said, QUIT MARKING ME!

MARKER: What a fuss budget. I like marking. It makes me feel important.

BOOKER: Well, you are not going to mark me. *(Pushes MARKER off the library shelf.)*

BOOKWORM: Good work, Booker.

BOOKER: Thanks, Bookworm. Say, it is almost time for _____ (librarian's name) to arrive, and then, the children. How I love the children.

BOOKWORM: I love the children, too, and I love living here in the library. I think your library party will be wonderfully beau-u-tiful, and divine.

BOOKER: I think so, too.

ROARY: *(Enters and whispers.)* Booker?

BOOKER: What are you whispering for, Bookworm?

BOOKWORM: I'm not whispering. I'm talking softly, like we always do in the library.

BOOKER: Then, who is whispering?

ROARY: I'm whispering. Roary, the lion, is whispering. If I promise not to roar in the library, can I come to your party?

BOOKER: Roary, you don't have to whisper, just talk softly.

Booker's Library Party

ROARY: *(Talks softly.)* If I talk softly, can I come to your library party? Please?

BOOKER: Well—

BOOKWORM: You promise to talk softly all the time you are in the library?

ROARY: I promise.

BOOKER: Well, O.K., you can come.

ROARY: Thanks, Booker. I'll go and comb my mane so I'll be ready for the party. *(Leaves.)*

BOOKER: Roary is a real, nice lion.

BOOKWORM: He is, when he's not roaring.

STICKY ICKY: *(Enters.)* Booker?

BOOKWORM: Oh, no! Not you, again.

STICKY ICKY: I am talking to Booker. I want to ask you a question, Booker.

BOOKER: *(Backs away from* STICKY ICKY.*)* O.K., but stay away from me.

STICKY ICKY: If I wash my hands, can I come to the party?

BOOKER: Well—

STICKY ICKY: Please, Booker?

BOOKER: Well, O.K., if you wash your hands real good.

STICKY ICKY: Oh, I will, Booker. Real good! *(Leaves.)*

BOOKER: Sticky Icky is nice.

BOOKWORM: She is, when she's not sticky.

MARKER: *(Enters.)* I say, Booker.

BOOKWORM: *(Moves to* MARKER.*)* Don't you go marking my friend.

MARKER: Booker, if I promise I will not mark you, not one little mark, can I come to your library party? What do you say, Booker, old chap?

BOOKER: Well—

MARKER: I will put my marker away, if you do.

BOOKER: Well, O.K. You can come to my library party if you put your marker away.

MARKER: That's jolly good. I'll be back directly. I'll just take my marker home. *(Leaves.)*

BOOKWORM: I never thought I'd see the day you'd invite Roary, Sticky Icky and Marker to your library party.

BOOKER: I never thought so either, Bookworm.

LIBRARIAN: *(Enters.)* Hello, Booker. Is everything ready for the party?

BOOKER: Yes, _____ (librarian's name). Everything is ready. I picked out the book for you to read at the party. It's a good one.

BOOKWORM: And, wait until you see the bookmarks and paper chains that everyone is going to make, designed by Booker.

LIBRARIAN: It sounds wonderful.

BOOKWORM: And, bea-u-tiful and divine.

BOOKER: And, we're having CHUG CHUG juice, and Whistle-Stop cookies. You have to whistle before you can have a cookie. *(Whistles.)*

BOOKWORM: Won't it be a super party? Didn't Booker plan a perfect party?

LIBRARIAN: Yes, he did. The children will love it. I hear them now. *(Turns to the children in the audience.)* Hello, everyone. Welcome to Booker's Library Party. First I will read you Booker's Book. Then we will have the party. *(A book is read, followed by a party.)*

Props: Lollipop; yellow marker.

Production Note: The party can be tailored to the needs of the librarian. If not available, the refreshments can be left out.

Bookmarks

Bookmarks can be made from colored construction paper. The children can color designs on them and write their names. (Librarian can help the younger children with their names.) The librarian can explain how bookmarks protect a book.

Paper Chains

Paper chains are fun and easy to make. Cut strips of colored construction paper and place in center of table. Show the children how to loop the paper in a circle. Scotch tape or glue the first circle. Then show how you stick another strip of paper through the first circle, glue this strip into a circle, and keep adding circles. Depending on the time, bracelets or necklaces can be made, or a long chain put together with everyone's chains to decorate the library. Use narrow strips for necklaces and bracelets, and wider strips for room decorations.

Things to Remember

Keep your eyes on your puppet.

Keep puppets at a constant height while performing.

When one puppet is speaking, the other puppets are still.

Make scenery and props simple.

Do not have too many puppets on the stage at one time.

Learn all cues for exits and entrances.

Take good care of your puppets — stuff with tissue paper and cover with plastic bag when not in use.

If you leave a prop on the stage, forget a line, the lights go out, or the mike squawks, cover these mistakes with puppet talk or action.

If you are using a mouth puppet, keep the mouth closed when not talking, and when talking, synchronize the mouth action with the dialogue. Practice before a mirror.

Know your script well, and have as many rehearsals as necessary to give a smooth performance.

Be sure your puppet's costume does not clash with the scenery, or be lost against it.

If possible, add suitable music to a performance either with records, a children's band, or piano. Music sets the mood.

Have an emergency kit handy with things you might need such as: flashlight, scotch tape, hammer, nails, extension cord, scissors, pins, pencil, etc.

Be sure to have as much action as possible in the play. Keep intermissions between acts short.

Simple Puppet Stages

Puppet stages don't have to be expensive or specially built. A very nice stage for beginners can be improvised in any number of ways. The ideas on the following pages are meant for use as hand puppet stages, although the first two could also be used as shadow puppet stages with the addition of a screen. Nancy Henk is the source of the ideas and drawings.

1. CARDBOARD STAGE

Cut a stage opening in a large cardboard box or packing crate.

Simple Puppet Stages

Inside view

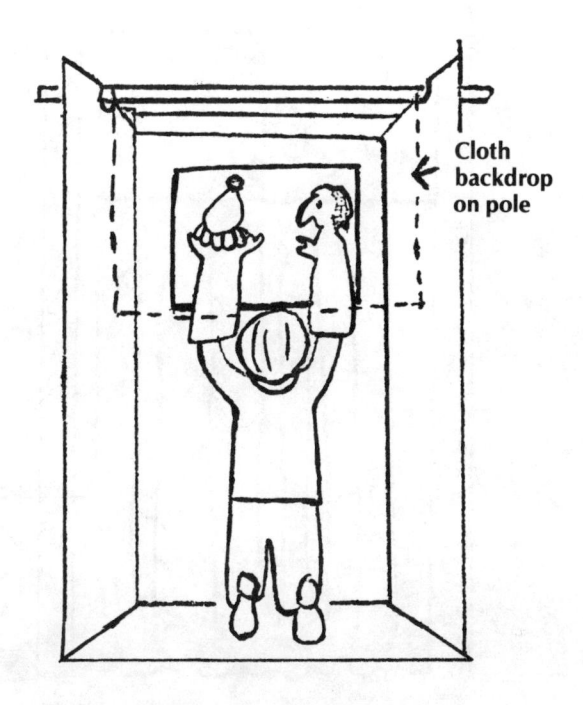

← Cloth backdrop on pole

Leave bottom of box in.

2. DOORWAY WITH CURTAIN

Puppeteer works standing.

Curtain can be supported by a tension rod – about $1 at most variety stores.

Simple Puppet Stages 131

3. BLANKET

A sheet or blanket can be attached to a broomstick and held by 2 persons. Very good for outdoor puppet shows.

4. IRONING BOARD

A sheet or blanket can be draped over an ironing board. This makes a nice shelf for props.

5. CARD TABLE

Put one table resting on its side with two legs extended on top of another cardtable. The front may be draped if desired.